hamlyn

Juices, smoothies, coolers, infusions and soups

100 HEALTH-BOOSTING
DRINKS

An Hachette UK company
www.hachette.co.uk

First published in Great Britain in 2005 by
Hamlyn, a division of Octopus Publishing Group Ltd
Carmelite House
50 Victoria Embankment
London, EC4Y 0DZ
www.octopusbooksusa.com

This edition published in 2015

Distributed in the US by
Hachette Book Group
1290 Avenue of the Americas
4th and 5th Floors
New York, NY 10020

Distributed in Canada by
Canadian Manda Group
664 Annette Street
Toronto, Ontario, Canada M6S 2C8

ISBN 978-0-600-63066-1

Printed and bound in China

10 9 8 7 6 5 4 3 2 1

All reasonable care has been taken in the preparation
of this book but the information it contains is not
intended to take the place of treatment by a qualified
medical practitioner.

Contents

introduction

We know we should eat five portions of fruits and vegetables a day, but few of us do. *100 Health-Boosting Drinks* will show you how to get the fruit and vegetables you need in a delicious and nutritious form.

What are health-boosting drinks?

They are juices, smoothies, coolers, infusions and soups made from nutritious ingredients and designed to maintain optimum health.

JUICES are simple to make with a juicer using just about any fruit or vegetable.

SMOOTHIES are juices or whole pieces of fruit blended to make thicker drinks.

COOLERS are tall, refreshing drinks often made with sparkling water and usually served over ice.

INFUSIONS are made with boiling water. The nutrients can be easily absorbed when drunk.

SOUPS offer a comforting way to eat plenty of ingredients with health-giving properties.

How do they benefit health?

The main benefits of health-boosting drinks are the vitamins, minerals and enzymes contained in the fruits and vegetables. As the produce is generally in a raw state, nearly all of the nutrients are retained.

● **PROTECTION AGAINST DISEASE** A diet rich in fruit and vegetables can prevent and help to cure a range of ailments. Phytochemicals from plants hold the key to preventing some of our most deadly diseases such as heart disease and cancer as well as other ailments and allergies.

● **IMMUNITY BOOSTING** Vegetables and fruit are sources of nutrients, such as vitamins C and E, betacarotene and minerals. These help to keep you in tiptop health and boost your immunity so you don't succumb to every virus around.

● **ENERGY ENHANCING** These drinks keep you feeling full longer than "empty" snacks like crisps and chocolate. The nutrients in them give you an energy boost, and if you consume them regularly, you will have noticeably more energy.

● **EXTRA FLUIDS** Water is vital for health. It makes up more than 65 percent of our cells, and as much as 80 percent of some brain cells. These drinks contain plenty of fluids and don't have the dehydrating effects of tea, coffee and soft drinks.

● **ANTI-AGING BENEFITS** The antioxidants in fruits and vegetables are nature's secret weapons against aging and have been found to protect against wrinkles, sagging skin, loss of muscle tone, age spots and the onset of many age-related diseases.

- **DETOX** Many of the drinks in this book have a detox effect, helping to clear toxins in the body, leaving you refreshed and rejuvenated.
- **WEIGHT LOSS** Health-boosting drinks are great in a weight-loss program as they are satisfying and nutritious. However, be sure to include a balance of foods to maintain healthy cells.

Choosing ingredients

Choose the freshest ingredients as nutrients disappear after fruits and vegetables are picked. Frozen fruits and vegetables are a good second choice if they have been frozen immediately after picking. They often contain more vitamins and minerals than fresh produce past its prime.

Buying organic

Many people prefer to buy organic, and research has shown that levels of zinc, vitamin C and carotene are higher in organic produce. Another advantage is that many non-organic fruits and vegetables contain pesticides and do not need to be peeled before being eaten. As most enzymes, vitamins and minerals lie just below the surface of the skin, peeling is counterproductive. It is much better to buy organic. Scrub all fruits and vegetables under warm running water.

Making juices

You will need an electric juicer to separate the juice from the pulp. There are two basic types: centrifugal juicers and masticating juicers. Centrifugal juicers are widely available and

affordable while masticating juicers extract a little more juice but are more expensive. Choose a model that is easy to clean and that takes relatively large pieces of fruits and vegetable to reduce the amount of chopping and the time it takes to feed the produce through the machine.

Cut foods into manageable pieces including the skin and seeds if the produce is organic or has been thoroughly scrubbed. Don't include the skin of pineapple, mango, papaya, orange, lemon or banana and remove pits from apricots, peaches, mangoes, avocados and plums.

key ingredients

ingredient	nutrients	benefits
Almonds	Calcium, magnesium, phosphorus, zinc, potassium, folic acid, vitamins B12, B3, E	Reduce risk of heart disease, lower cholesterol, anticancer
Apple	Calcium, vitamin C, magnesium, beta-carotene, pectin	Cleansing, high fiber, antioxidant, anti-inflammatory, lowers cholesterol, anticancer, counters diarrhea and constipation, helps joint problems, prevents disease
Apricot	Beta-carotene, iron, potassium, folic acid, boron, copper, calcium, vitamin C	Regulates blood pressure, soluble fiber, antioxidant
Asparagus	Potassium, folic acid, beta-carotene, vitamins C, K	Mild laxative, stimulates the kidneys, antibacterial
Avocado	Vitamins E, C, B6, potassium, folic acid, iron	Reduces cholesterol and atherosclerosis, antioxidant, easy on digestion, balances acid–alkaline content
Banana	Potassium, vitamins B6, C, tryptophan, beta-carotene	Maintains bowel health, boosts blood sugar levels, promotes sleep, lowers cholesterol, natural antibiotic
Barley	Calcium, iron, magnesium, zinc, folic acid, potassium, phosphorus, B vitamins	Lowers estrogen levels, soluble fiber, may help to avoid heart disease, heals stomach ulcers
Beet	Calcium, magnesium, iron, potassium, folic acid, vitamin C	Cleansing, fortifies blood, eliminates kidney stones, detoxifies the liver
Black pepper	Calcium, magnesium, potassium, manganese, phosphorus	Digestive stimulant, antioxidant, antibacterial
Blackberries	Beta-carotene, vitamins C and E, calcium, magnesium, phosphorus, potassium, sodium	Antioxidant, boost immune system, anti-aging
Blueberries	Vitamin C, beta-carotene	Antioxidant, anti-inflammatory, anticoagulant, combats diarrhea, antibacterial, anti-aging
Broccoli	Folic acid, betacarotene, magnesium, calcium, vitamins C, B3, B5, phosphorus	Anticancer, antioxidant, antibiotic, antiviral, cleanses liver and intestines
Cabbage	Calcium, magnesium, vitamins C, E, K, folic acid, potassium, beta-carotene	Detoxifies colon, antiviral, supports immune system, antioxidant, antibacterial, relieves gastric ulcers

Carrot	Beta-carotene, calcium, potassium, magnesium	Detoxifier, supports liver and digestive tract, antibacterial, antiviral
Celery	Folic acid, vitamin B3, sodium, potassium	Anticancer, lowers blood pressure, diuretic, anti-inflammatory
Cilantro	Vitamin C, potassium	Good for circulatory system, digestive system and the skin, relieves migraines
Cinnamon	Calcium, iron, potassium	Stimulates digestive system, relieves nausea
Coconut	Magnesium, potassium, phosphorus, zinc, folic acid, vitamin C	Regulates thyroid function
Cranberries	Potassium, beta-carotene, vitamin C	Reduce bladder infections, help to maintain a healthy heart, anti-inflammatory, antiviral, antibacterial
Cucumber	Potassium, beta-carotene	Diuretic, lowers blood pressure, benefits kidneys
Fennel	Folic acid, sodium, vitamin C, calcium, magnesium, potassium	Antispasmodic, rebalances hormones in menopausal women, helps break down fat
Garlic	Calcium, potassium, vitamin C, allicin	Antibacterial, antiviral, antiseptic, lowers cholesterol, thins blood, supports immune system
Ginger	Calcium, magnesium, potassium	Antispasmodic, alleviates nausea and menstrual cramps, relieves indigestion and flatulence, discourages blood clots, stimulates circulation
Grapefruit	Calcium, magnesium, potassium, vitamin C	May reduce the risk of some cancers, helps arthritis, improves blood circulation, lowers cholesterol levels
Grapes	Glucose, fructose, potassium, vitamin C, carotene	Fights carcinogens, relieves arthritis, lowers blood pressure and helps urinary disorders
Horseradish	Vitamin C, potassium	Improves circulation, regulates blood pressure, relieves flu symptoms, lowers cholesterol, anticancer
Lemons/limes	Potassium, vitamin C	Lower cholesterol, anticancer
Lentils	Iron, potassium, folate, zinc, B vitamins	Control blood sugar, lower cholestrol, aid bowel health
Mango	Vitamin C, beta-carotene	Supports kidneys, aids digestion, good blood cleanser
Melon	Calcium, potassium, vitamin C, beta-carotene	Anticoagulant, lowers heart disease risk, cleanses and rehydrates
Mushrooms	Zinc, calcium, iron, magnesium, folic acid, B vitamins	Lower cholesterol, support immune function
Onions	Quercetin, folic acid, potassium, calcium, beta-carotene, magnesium	Reduce risk of heart disease, anticancer, relieve congestion in airways

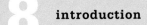 **introduction**

Oranges	Vitamin C, beta-carotene, folic acid, calcium, potassium	Reduce risk of some cancers, improve circulation, lower cholesterol, stimulate, cleanse, internal antiseptic
Papaya	Vitamin C, beta-carotene, calcium, potassium	Aids digestion, soothes internal inflammation, antiparasitic, anticancer, a great detoxifier
Parsley	Folate, vitamin C, iron, calcium	Antioxidant, strengthens, thins and cleanses blood, diuretic, helps kidney function and eases gout
Parsnips	Folate, potassium, vitamins C, E	Fiber, help maintain blood pressure, strengthen blood
Peaches	Carotenes, flavonoids and vitamin C	Good for irritated stomachs and persistent coughs, lower blood pressure, protect against heart disease, anticancer
Pears	Potassium, beta-carotene, vitamin C	Steady release of sugar maintains blood sugar levels
Peppers	Potassium, betacarotene, folic acid, vitamin C	Antibacterial, regulate blood pressure, good for circulation, stimulate gastric juices and peristalsis
Pineapple	Vitamin C, bromelain, potassium, beta-carotene	Anticoagulant, aids digestion
Raspberries	Ellagic acid, magnesium, potassium, vitamin C	Regulate menstrual cycle, antiviral, help weight loss
Soy milk (plain, unfortified)	Protein, iron, calcium, vitamins D, B12	Reduces risk of heart disease and cancer, lowers cholesterol, helps some menopausal symptoms
Spinach	Potassium, folate, iron, vitamins B, C, beta-carotene	Anticancer, strengthens blood, may protect against eye degeneration and heart disease
Strawberries	Vitamins A, C, K, betacarotene, folic acid, potassium	Antioxidant, anticancer, antiviral, antibacterial
Sweet potato	Beta-carotene, vitamins C, E, folic acid, calcium, magnesium, potassium	Aids heart health, antioxidants, helps regulate high blood pressure, anti-inflammatory, strengthens blood
Tofu	Iron, protein, potassium, magnesium, calcium, vitamins A, K	Lowers risk of some cancers, helps prevent osteoporosis, controls diabetes and symptoms of the menopause
Tomatoes	Calcium, magnesium, phosphorus, beta-carotene, folic acid, vitamin C	May reduce risk of prostate and breast cancer, antiseptic, anti-inflammatory
Wheat	Calcium, iron, magnesium, potassium, phosphorus, zinc, folic acid, manganese, vitamins B5, B6	Organic, untreated whole wheat with bran and germ left intact stimulates the liver and eliminates toxins
Yogurt	Calcium, vitamin D	Soothes intestinal tract, promotes good bacteria

rda table

vitamin/rda	function	food sources
vitamin A (retinol) 600 mcg	Promotes eye health; antioxidant with immunity-boosting function	Liver, dairy products, eggs, oily fish
beta-carotene (pro-vitamin A) 25 mg	Antioxidant, anticancer; the body can convert beta-carotene into vitamin A	All dark green, orange or red fruits and vegetables, e.g., red pepper, pumpkin and spinach
vitamin B1 (thiamine) 0.8 mg	Needed for energy production and for a healthy nervous system	Milk, meat, whole grain/fortified breakfast cereals, dried fruits, nuts, brown rice, peas and beans
vitamin B2 (riboflavin) 1.3 mg	Helps the body get energy from food; aids healthy eyes, hair and nails	Milk, liver, kidneys, cheese, fortified breakfast cereals
vitamin B5 (pantothenic acid) No official RDA	Anti-stress vitamin, boosting the metabolism and aiding energy release from food	Liver, kidneys, yeast, wheat germ, fortified breakfast cereals, whole grain bread, nuts, legumes, fresh vegetables
vitamin B6 (pyridoxine) 1.2 mg	Balances hormonal change in women and helps cell production	Numerous foods, including meat, whole grain bread, brown rice, bananas and legumes
vitamin B12 (cobaldmin) 1.5 mg	Aids red blood cell production and maintenance of healthy nerves	Liver, kidney, oily fish, meat, eggs, dairy products, fortified breakfast cereals
folic acid 200 mg	Prevention of spinal disabilities in the fetus; aids red blood cell production and energy release from food	Green leafy vegetables, liver, pulses, eggs, whole grain cereals, orange juice, wheat germ
vitamin C (ascorbic acid) 40 mg	Protects against some cancers and coronary heart disease; helps maintain healthy bones, teeth and gums	Most fruits and vegetables—among the best sources are kiwi fruits, citrus fruits, peppers, currants and strawberries
vitamin D (calciferol) 10 mg	Promotes a healthy nervous system; formation of healthy bones and teeth	Oily fish, dairy products, eggs
vitamin E (tocopherols) 10 mg	Antioxidant; protects against heart disease and cancer	Vegetable oils, polyunsaturated margarine, wheat germ, sunflower seeds, hazelnuts, oily fish, whole grain cereal, eggs, avocado and spinach
vitamin K 10 mg	Necessary in the formation of blood clots when the body needs it	Broccoli, cabbage, spinach, liver, alfafa, tomatoes and kelp

ailment chart

ailment	recommended recipes
Acid stomach	Digestive Duo, Fiery Indian Broth, Herbal Harmony, Tropicana, Tummy Tonic
Allergies	Caribbean Spice, Eat Your Greens
Anemia	Beet This, Blood Orange, Chill-Out, Pecan Punch, Red Devil, Red Wire, Squeaky Green
Arthritis	Acher Shaker, Bean Good, Brain Booster, Caribbean Spice, Chill-Out, Karma Kooler, Twister, Zesty Ginger Beer
Asthma	Classic C & C, Hot Stuff, Lentil Power
Bloating/ water retention	Black-Eyed Pea Bonanza, Cabbage Soup, Dynamic Detox, Evergreen, Feel-Good Fennel, Flush-a-Bye-Baby, Ginger Zinger, Herbal Harmony, The Great Gazpacho
Bronchitis	Citrus Squeeze, Hot Stuff, The Great Gazpacho
Cellulite	Bumpy Ride, Feel-Good Fennel, The Great Gazpacho
Cholesterol reduction	Belly Berry, Black-Eyed Pea Bonanza, Brain Booster, Chill-out, Lentil Power, Purple Passion, Wild Mushroom Dream
Colds and flu	Berry Nice, C for Comfort, Classic C & C, Frisky Sour, Ginger Zinger, Hot Stuff, Passion Fruit Plus, Sweet Stinger, Orient Express
Constipation	Black-Eyed Pea Bonanza, Cabbage Soup, Feel-Good Fennel, Summer Soup, The Great Gazpacho, Way to Go
Cystitis	Cleansing Cranberry, Flush-a-Bye-Baby, Smooth and Soothing
Detox	Digestive Duo, Dynamic Detox, Flush-a-Bye-Baby, Freshen Up, Herbal Harmony, Herbi-four, Juicy Lucy, Lemon Barley Water, Orchard Medley, Red Devil, Spring Clean, Squeaky Green, Strawberry Cleanser, Tropical Trio
Diarrhoea	Belly Berry, Purple Passion, Zesty Ginger Beer
Dieting	Cool and Cleansing, Evergreen, Flush-a-Bye-Baby, Ginger Spice, Karma Kooler
Eczema	Cabbage Soup, Classic C & C
Eyesight	Berry Mull, Caribbean Spice, Carroty Cooler, Chunky Chowder, Classic C & C, Papaya Flyer, Seeing Red, Twister, Vision Impeccable

Hemorrhoids	Brain Booster, Summer Soup, Way to Go
Hangover	Beet This, Classic C & C, Full Tank, Hot Stuff, Karma Kooler, Morning After, Orient Express, Warm and Spicy, Zesty Ginger Beer
Headaches and migraines	Brain Booster, Evergreen, Fever Fusion, The Great Gazpacho
Heart disease	Brain Booster, Bumpy Ride, Classic C & C
High blood pressure	Fruity Filler, Lounge Lizard, Plum Punch, The Great Gazpacho
Hypoglycaemia	Black-Eyed Pea Bonanza, Chill-out, Chunky Chowder, Minty Magic
Immune system	Frisky Sour, Ginger Zinger, Golden Fizz, Mango Magic, Morning After, Passion Fruit Plus, Protein Pack, Quick Hit, Sergeant Pepper, Tchae Trio, Time Out, Tomato Tonic, What's Up Broc?
Insomnia	Pillow Talk, Sleeping Beauty, Sleep Tight, Smooth Operator, Soothing Brew
Irritable Bowel Syndrome	Mussel Power, Spring Clean
Lethargy	Power Pack, Juicy Lucy, Vitamin Vitality, Energy Bubble, Red Wire, Tongue Tingler
Low energy	Brain Booster, Energy Fizz, Feel-Good Fennel, High Kick, Rose Royce, Time Out, The Great Gazpacho
Low fertility	Green Dream, Mussel Power, Passion Thriller, Tofu and Papaya Soup
Menopause	Brain Booster, Eat Your Greens, Mussel Power
Osteoporosis	Chill-Out, Lentil Power, Mango Magic, Minty Magic, Caribbean Spice, Fiery Indian Broth
PMS	Brain Booster, Caribbean Spice, Sleep Tight
Pregnancy care	Squeaky Green
Seasonal Affective Disorder	Berried Treasure, Black Bean Bonanza, Chunky Veggie Chowder, Recovery, Smooth and Soothing, Smooth Operator, Brain Booster
Sinusitis	Ginger Spice, Hot Stuff, Lentil Power
Skin disorders	Beauty Fuel, Carroty Cooler, Green Dream, Herbi-Four, Passion Thriller, Peach Dream, Protein Pack, Sour Power
Stress	Evergreen, Feelin' Good, Feel-Good Fennel, Hula Kula, Lounge Lizard, Papaya Flyer, Pillow Talk, Smooth Operator, Soothing Brew
Weight gain	Eat Your Greens, Feel-Good Fennel, Green Dream, Minty Magic, Orient Express, Passion Thriller, Sweet Chariot

11

frisky sour

½ **small (5 oz) papaya**

½ **medium (5 oz) grapefruit**

½ **pint (5 oz) raspberries**

½ **lime, plus slices to decorate**

ice cubes

A great tonic for colds and flu. If you're run down and haven't been eating a balanced diet, your immune system becomes more susceptible—try this.

1 Scoop out the papaya flesh and juice it with the grapefruit (with the pith left on) and the raspberries.

2 Squeeze in the juice of the lime and mix. Serve with ice cubes and decorate with lime slices.

makes 1 cup (8 fl oz)

NUTRITIONAL CONTENT: **energy** 152 cals | **calcium** 110 mg | **magnesium** 55 mg | **zinc** 1.1 mg | **vitamin C** 219 mg | **vitamin A** 183 mcg.

13

sergeant pepper

½ **medium (3½ oz) red pepper**

½ **medium (3½ oz) yellow pepper**

½ **medium (3½ oz) orange pepper**

1 orange

1 tablespoon mint leaves

ice cubes

Another good choice if you're run down and fighting a cold or flu. Peppers ward off infection and are natural painkillers.

1 Juice the peppers and orange and serve in a tumbler with ice cubes. Stir in the mint leaves.

makes 1 cup (8 fl oz)

NUTRITIONAL CONTENT: energy 130 cals | **calcium** 91 mg | **magnesium** 58 mg | **zinc** 0.4 mg | **vitamin C** 466 mg | **vitamin A** 714 mcg.

15

NUTRITIONAL CONTENT: energy 99 cals I **calcium** 86 mg I **magnesium** 39 mg I **zinc** 0.2 mg I **vitamin C** 84 mg I **vitamin A** 108 mcg.

2 small (4 oz) carrots

¼ small (8 oz) cantaloupe

1 lime, plus wedges to serve

1-inch cube of fresh ginger, roughly chopped

seeds from 1 cardamom pod

ice cubes

A juice rich in antioxidants. The lime encourages the elimination of toxins.

1 Juice the carrots, cantaloupe, lime and ginger. Serve in a glass over ice. Decorate with lime wedges and seeds from the cardamom pod.

makes 1 cup (8 fl oz)

ginger zinger

what's up broc?

1 head (8 oz) broccoli

3 small (6 oz) carrots

1 small (2 oz) beet

1 cilantro sprig, to decorate

Broccoli is a natural antibiotic and is also powerfully anti-viral, providing an instant boost to your immune system.

1 Juice the broccoli, carrots and beet and serve in a tall glass. Decorate with a cilantro sprig.

makes 1 cup (8 fl oz)

NUTRITIONAL CONTENT: energy 153 cals | **calcium** 210 mg | **magnesium** 76 mg | **zinc** 2.1 mg | **vitamin C** 227 mg | **vitamin A** 1796 mcg.

19

time out

¼ pint (3½ oz) fresh or frozen blackberries

¼ cantaloupe, rind removed

2 kiwi

Not just a great color, this juice is loaded with vitamin C, calcium and magnesium, essential for energy production and body cell maintenance.

1 Reserve a few blackberries for decoration, juice the remainder with the cantaloupe and kiwi, then put the juices in a blender and process with a couple of ice cubes. Pour into a glass and serve decorated with the reserved blackberries.

makes 1 cup (8 fl oz)

NUTRITIONAL CONTENT: **energy** 112 cals I **calcium** 101 mg I **magnesium** 58 mg I **zinc** 0.3 mg I **vitamin C** 125 mg I **vitamin A** 271 mcg.

21

protein pack

1 cup (5 oz) frozen mixed summer berries, plus extra to decorate

1 cup (8 fl oz) vanilla-flavored soy milk

1 teaspoon honey (optional)

A lovely summer drink rich in zinc and vitamin C, both great for warding off infections. To make it even more nutritious, use a soy milk enriched with calcium.

1 Place the berries, soy milk and honey, if using, in a blender and process until thick. Serve immediately, decorated with berries.

makes about 2 cups (14 fl oz)

NUTRITIONAL CONTENT: **energy** 202 cals I **calcium** 84 mg I **magnesium** 80 mg I **zinc** 1 mg I **vitamin C** 62 mg I **vitamin A** 8 mcg.

NUTRITIONAL CONTENT: **energy** 218 cals | **calcium** 74 mg | **magnesium** 68 mg | **zinc** 0.3 mg | **vitamin C** 296 mg | **vitamin A** 461 mcg.

⅓ **pint (4 oz) strawberries, hulled**

1 small ripe mango, peeled and pitted, plus extra slices to decorate

1 cup (8 fl oz) orange juice

Mango is rich in beta-carotene, a precursor of vitamin A. With the vitamin C from the orange juice and strawberries this drink gives a hit of antioxidants, protective against cancers.

1 Roughly chop the strawberries and the mango and freeze for at least 2 hours or overnight.

2 Place them in a blender with the orange juice and process until thick. Decorate with slices of mango.

makes about 2 cups (14 fl oz)

quick hit

mango magic

½ large mango, peeled

½ cup (4 fl oz) live yogurt

½ cup (4 fl oz) water

1 mint sprig, to decorate

A delicious creamy smoothie loaded with calcium for bones and blood, and rich in protective beta-carotene.

1 Blend the mango with the other ingredients until smooth, then serve decorated with a sprig of mint.

makes 1½ cups (12 fl oz)

NUTRITIONAL CONTENT: energy 99 cals I **calcium** 199 mg I **magnesium** 29 mg I **zinc** 0.7 mg I **vitamin C** 29 mg I **vitamin A** 234 mcg.

27

carroty cooler

¼ small (8 oz) cantaloupe, rind removed

1 cup (8 fl oz) carrot juice, chilled

½ cup (4 fl oz) orange juice

juice of 2 limes

ice cubes

A refreshing drink stacked with vitamin C and carotenes, the vitamin A precursors. Vitamin C acts as an internal antiseptic and is great for warding off infections.

1 Put the cantaloupe into a food processor or blender and process for 1 minute, then add the carrot, orange and lime juices and process again until thoroughly mixed. To serve, pour into tall glasses over crushed ice.

makes 2½ cups (20 fl oz)

NUTRITIONAL CONTENT: **energy** 80 cals I **calcium** 57 mg I **magnesium** 35 mg I **zinc** 0.2 mg I **vitamin C** 87 mg I **vitamin A** 1905 mcg.

29

tomato tonic

½ **cup (4 fl oz) tomato juice**

¼ **small cucumber, peeled**

2 dashes of lemon juice

2 dashes of Worcestershire sauce

salt and pepper

cucumber slice, to decorate

crushed ice

Tasty and refreshing for a hot day, this low-calorie drink supplies vitamin C and a range of other vitamins and minerals.

1 Put a little crushed ice into a blender. Add the tomato juice, cucumber, lemon juice, Worcestershire sauce and salt and pepper to taste and blend well.

2 Pour the drink into a cocktail glass and decorate with a slice of cucumber on the rim.

makes 1 cup (8 fl oz)

NUTRITIONAL CONTENT: **energy** 30 cals | **calcium** 39 mg | **magnesium** 25 mg | **zinc** 0.2 mg | **vitamin C** 16 mg | **vitamin A** 53 mcg.

31

NUTRITIONAL CONTENT: **energy** 98 cals I **calcium** 45 mg I **magnesium** 25 mg I **zinc** 0.5 mg I **vitamin C** 151 mg I **vitamin A** 151 mcg.

1 papaya, peeled, quartered and seeded

1 cup (8 fl oz) orange juice

sparkling mineral water

sprig of mint, to decorate

ice cubes

A golden cooler stuffed with vitamin C, vitamin A and beta-carotenes. It protects against infection and some cancers.

1 Place the papaya and orange juice in a food processor or blender and process for about 30 seconds until smooth.

2 Put 2–3 ice cubes into 2 tall glasses, pour in the drink and top up with sparkling water. Stir and decorate with a mint sprig.

makes 2 cups (16 fl oz)

golden fizz

sweet stinger

1 clementine

4 nettle sprigs

1 cup (8 fl oz) boiling water

honey, to sweeten

Gather fresh, young nettle leaves for this mild infusion. You'll need to wear gloves when picking the leaves, but the "sting" soon goes once the leaves are heated. Like citrus fruits, nettles are rich in vitamin C and minerals, giving your system an invigorating boost.

1 Pare a long strip of rind from the clementine, then halve it and squeeze the juice.

2 Put the clementine rind and nettle sprigs in a cup and cover with boiling water. Leave to infuse for 3–5 minutes.

3 Lift out the nettle sprigs and stir in the squeezed clementine juice and a little honey to sweeten.

makes 1 cup (8 fl oz)

NUTRITIONAL CONTENT: **energy** 39 cals | **calcium** 15 mg | **magnesium** 5 mg | **zinc** 0.1 mg | **vitamin C** 22 mg | **vitamin A** 8 mcg.

35

passion fruit plus

1 lemongrass stalk

1 cup (8 fl oz) boiling water

2 passion fruits

1 lime

2 teaspoons honey

This exotic infusion offers a warming way to get plenty of vitamin C. The lemongrass is fresh tasting and aromatic and, like passion fruit, has antiseptic properties.

1 Cut the lemongrass stalk in half lengthwise then finely chop one of the halves. Put in a small bowl and cover with boiling water. Leave to infuse for 3–4 minutes.

2 Halve the passion fruits and scoop the pulp into a tea strainer, set over a cup. Press the pulp with the back of a teaspoon to extract the juice.

3 Add the lime juice to the cup and strain in the lemongrass infusion through the strainer. Add the honey and use the halved lemongrass stalk as a stirrer.

makes 1 cup (8 fl oz)

NUTRITIONAL CONTENT: energy 71 cals I **calcium** 7 mg I **magnesium** 11 mg I **zinc** 0.5 mg I **vitamin C** 18 mg I **vitamin A** 38 mcg.

37

tchae trio

1 cup (8 fl oz) boiling water

1 green tea bag

2 large parsley sprigs

4 large pineapple sage leaves

2 lemon thyme sprigs

½ teaspoon honey

Try a double dose of immune-boosting nutrients with this combination of green tea and healing herbs. Parsley is rich in vitamins A, B and C and has diuretic and cleansing properties. Pineapple sage and lemon thyme are both antiseptic and give this infusion a fresh, tingly aftertaste.

1 Pour the boiling water over the tea bag in a cup and leave to infuse for 1 minute.

2 Lightly crush the parsley and sage leaves between your fingers to bruise them and release the flavor. Add to the cup with the thyme and honey. Leave for 3–4 minutes then drain the teabag and herbs.

makes 1 cup (8 fl oz)

NUTRITIONAL CONTENT: energy 27 cals | **calcium** 42 mg | **magnesium** 7 mg | **zinc** 0.1 mg | **vitamin C** 11 mg | **vitamin A** 64 mcg.

39

the great gazpacho

2 lbs ripe yellow tomatoes, skinned, seeded and chopped

½ cucumber, peeled, seeded and chopped

2 yellow peppers, cored, seeded and chopped

2 garlic cloves, crushed

1 small onion, roughly chopped

6 basil leaves, plus extra to garnish

2 tablespoons white wine vinegar

½ cup (4 fl oz) olive oil

1 cup (8 fl oz) vegetable stock

1 tablespoon lemon juice

Tabasco sauce (optional)

salt and pepper

to garnish

¼ cup Greek yogurt

¼ cup finely diced red pepper or red chilies

The vibrant color of this delicious soup tells you that it is full of vitamin C, a natural antihistamine, making it a good anti-inflammatory choice for hayfever sufferers.

1 In a large bowl, mix together the tomatoes, cucumber, peppers, garlic, onion, basil, vinegar and olive oil and season well. Cover and leave in a cool place overnight.

2 The next day, add the stock and lemon juice and blend the mixture in a food processor until smooth. Transfer to a bowl, cover and chill.

3 Add a little Tabasco sauce if desired and season to taste. Pour the soup into chilled bowls and garnish with a spoonful of Greek yogurt, a sprinkling of red pepper or chilies and a few basil leaves.

serves 4

NUTRITIONAL CONTENT: energy 280 cals I **protein** 6 g I **fat** 24 g I **carbohydrate** 12 g I calcium 100 mg I **iron** 1.6 mg I **vitamin C** 103 mg.

NUTRITIONAL CONTENT: **energy** 224 cals | **protein** 6 g | **fat** 17 g | **carbohydrate** 13 g | **calcium** 20 mg | **iron** 0.9 mg | **vitamin C** 6 mg.

12 oz fresh wild mushrooms, such as morels, shiitake or oyster

1 tablespoon olive oil

1 onion, roughly chopped

1 potato, finely diced

4 cups (32 fl oz) chicken stock

2 garlic cloves, crushed

1½ cloves (12 fl oz) reduced-fat sour cream or crème fraîche

salt and pepper

This healthy soup is ideal for people with high cholesterol, as both mushrooms and garlic are well-known blood thinners. Shiitake mushrooms also have potent anticancer properties.

1 Chop the mushrooms very finely, reserving a few whole ones for garnish.

2 Pour half of the oil into a heavy saucepan and cook the onion and potato gently for 10 minutes or until the onion is translucent and the potato cooked through. Transfer to a food processor, cover with some of the stock and blend until smooth.

3 Put the chopped and whole mushrooms and garlic into the pan with the rest of the oil and sauté them gently for about 5 minutes. Add the remaining stock and bring to a boil then simmer for two minutes. Reserve the whole mushrooms.

4 Stir the potato mixture into the sour cream in a large bowl. Remove the soup from the heat and briskly stir a ladleful into the sour cream mixture. Add another couple of ladlefuls, and stir carefully. Return to the pan and mix. Place the pan on a very low heat and reheat gently. Season to taste and serve in warmed bowls, garnished with the reserved mushrooms.

serves 4

wild mushroom dream

boost your immunity: soups

classic c & c

1 tablespoon olive oil

2 bay leaves

1 onion, roughly chopped

2 garlic cloves, chopped

1¼ lbs carrots, roughly chopped

1 small bunch of cilantro, leaves separated from stems

5 cups (40 fl oz) vegetable stock

½ teaspoon garam masala

salt and pepper

¼ cup Greek yogurt or soy cream, to garnish

Carrots help to kill bacteria and viruses, so are an essential immune-boosting ingredient. There is a lot to be said for the old adage that carrots help you see in the dark—they really do improve your eyesight.

1 Heat the oil in a saucepan, add the bay leaves, onion and garlic and fry for 2 minutes. Add the carrots, cilantro stems and stock and bring to a boil. Simmer until the carrots are completely cooked.

2 Let the soup cool slightly, then remove the bay leaves and purée the soup in a food processor until smooth. If you like a very smooth soup, strain the soup back into the saucepan through a fine sieve; if not, just pour it all back into the pan and reheat gently. Season with salt, pepper and garam masala.

3 Finely chop half the cilantro leaves and stir them into the soup. Serve the soup in warmed bowls and garnish each portion with a tablespoon of Greek yogurt swirled in and the remaining cilantro leaves.

serves 4

NUTRITIONAL CONTENT: energy 152 cals | **protein** 5 g | **fat** 9 g | **carbohydrate** 17 g | **calcium** 122 mg | **iron** 1 mg | **vitamin C** 13 mg.

simply strawberry

1¾ lbs strawberries, hulled

⅓ cup (3 fl oz) orange juice

⅓ cup (3 fl oz) white grape juice

⅓ cup (3 oz) honey

2 tablespoons cornstarch

50 ml (2 fl oz) cold water

1 teaspoon lemon juice

amaretto biscotti, broken,
to decorate

Strawberries are antiviral, antibacterial and full of vitamin C, and they raise the levels of antioxidants in the body. This soup is a light, immune-boosting and luxurious way to finish a meal.

1 Blend the strawberries in a food processor then pass the purée through a sieve to remove the seeds.

2 Combine the orange and grape juices, honey and sieved strawberries in a saucepan and heat gently until the honey has dissolved.

3 Mix the cornstarch with the water and beat until no lumps remain. Pour into the hot soup, stirring continuously until the soup thickens. Add lemon juice to taste. Pour the soup into small bowls and decorate with the chunks of amaretto biscotti.

serves 4

NUTRITIONAL CONTENT: energy 152 cals | **calcium** 110 mg | **magnesium** 55 mg | **zinc** 1.1 mg | **vitamin C** 219 mg | **vitamin A** 183 mcg.

NUTRITIONAL CONTENT: energy 211 cals | **calcium** 164 mg | **magnesium** 46 mg | **zinc** 1 mg | **vitamin C** 182 mg | **vitamin A** 3393 mcg.

1 orange

4 small (8 oz) carrots

2 small (4 oz) beets

⅓ pint (4 oz) strawberries, hulled

ice cubes

Carrots, beets and oranges are all rich in vitamins A and C, antioxidants and phytonutrients such as alpha- and beta-carotene. This juice is also a rich source of potassium— a real tonic.

1 Reserve a few strips of orange peel for decoration, then juice the carrots, beets and orange. Put the juice into a blender with a couple of ice cubes and the strawberries.

2 Blend for 20 seconds and serve in a tall glass, decorated with strips of orange rind.

makes 1 cup (8 fl oz)

power pack

50

NUTRITIONAL CONTENT: energy 106 cals I **calcium** 125 mg I **magnesium** 26 mg I **zinc** 0.3 mg I **vitamin C** 133 mg I **vitamin A** 687 mcg.

2 oranges

1 carrot

ice cubes

A great juice to get you going in the morning, with lots of vitamin C and beta-carotene. The oranges provide calcium and magnesium, vital for body-cell repair.

1 Cut a slice from one of the oranges and set aside. Remove the peel from both oranges, leaving the pith in place. Juice the carrot with the oranges and serve over ice decorated with the reserved slice of orange.

makes 1 cup (8 fl oz)

vitamin vitality

energy bubble

3 apples, preferably red, plus slices to decorate

1 mango, peeled and pitted

2 passion fruits

ice cubes

Yellow-fleshed mango is high in beta-carotene, important in preventing some cancers. The apples and passion fruit add a healthy burst of vitamin C to get that energy going.

1 Juice the apples and mango with the passion fruit. Pour the juice into a glass and add a couple of ice cubes. Decorate with apple slices.

makes 1 cup (8 fl oz)

NUTRITIONAL CONTENT: energy 249 cals | **calcium** 33 mg | **magnesium** 43 mg | **zinc** 0.4 mg | **vitamin C** 71 mg | **vitamin A** 497 mcg.

53

red wire

½ **cup (4 oz) red grapes**

2 small beets (4 oz)

2 small plums, pitted, plus wedges to decorate

A colorful and attractive juice high in folate from the beets. The grapes and plums make it naturally sweet, giving an instant energy kick.

1 Juice the grapes, beets and plums together and serve in a tumbler over ice. Decorate with plum wedges.

makes 1 cup (8 fl oz)

NUTRITIONAL CONTENT: **energy** 116 cals | **calcium** 40 mg | **magnesium** 22 mg | **zinc** 0.6 mg | **vitamin C** 10 mg | **vitamin A** 34 mcg.

55

bionic tonic

1 large banana

1 large ripe mango, peeled and pitted

½ cup live yogurt

1 cup (8 fl oz) pineapple juice

chunks of pineapple, to decorate

A scrumptious smoothie that is a small meal in itself. Yogurt supplies vital protein, calcium and magnesium, and the vitamins from the fruit make this an action-packed drink.

1 Slice the banana and roughly chop the mango. Freeze for at least 2 hours or overnight.

2 Place the frozen banana and mango in a blender with the yogurt and pineapple juice. Process until smooth, pour into a glass and decorate with pineapple chunks and a stirrer.

makes 2½ cups (20 fl oz)

NUTRITIONAL CONTENT: energy 407 cals I **calcium** 259 mg I **magnesium** 98 mg I **zinc** 1.3 mg I **vitamin C** 103 mg I **vitamin A** 503 mcg.

smooth and soothing

⅓ cup (1½ oz) dried cranberries,
plus extra for decoration

juice of ½ lemon

1 large banana

1 tablespoon sesame seeds

2 tablespoons Greek yogurt

1 cup (8 fl oz) milk

crushed ice

This smoothie is rich in calcium (vital for bones and body cell repair) and also has useful amounts of iron (good for blood) and zinc (essential for healing and repair of body tissue). The yogurt and banana make this quite a substantial drink, a small meal in itself.

1 Process the cranberries and lemon juice in a blender until the berries are finely chopped.

2 Add the banana and sesame seeds then purée, scraping the mixture down from the sides of the bowl if necessary.

3 Add the yogurt and milk, processing until smooth and frothy. Pour into a glass over crushed ice and decorate with the extra dried cranberries.

makes 1 cup (8 fl oz)

NUTRITIONAL CONTENT: energy 395 cals | **calcium** 476 mg | **magnesium** 120 mg | **zinc** 2.2 mg | **vitamin C** 36 mg | **vitamin A** 174 mcg.

59

NUTRITIONAL CONTENT: energy 220 cals | calcium 73 mg | magnesium 68 mg | zinc 0.4 mg | vitamin C 235 mg | vitamin A 1005 mcg.

⅔ **pint (8 oz) strawberries, hulled**

1 kiwi

½ **large banana**

1 tablespoon spirulina

1 tablespoon linseeds

ice cubes

to decorate

1 tablespoon linseeds

1 sprig fresh currants

Spirulina is a green powder made from seaweed and is high in calcium, magnesium and vitamin A to give this smoothie a really high kick.

1 Juice the strawberries and kiwi, then process the juice in a blender with the banana, spirulina, linseeds and a couple of ice cubes. Pour into a glass and decorate with currants and linseeds.

makes 1 cup (8 fl oz)

high kick

NUTRITIONAL CONTENT: energy 95 cals | **calcium** 81 mg | **magnesium** 28 mg | **zinc** 0.4 mg | **vitamin C** 150 mg | **vitamin A** 8 mcg.

⅓ **pint (4 oz) strawberries, hulled**

½ **cup (3 oz) currants, plus extra to decorate**

½ **orange**

½ **cup (4 fl oz) water**

½ **teaspoon honey (optional)**

crushed ice

Colorful and cleansing, this refreshing drink packs a vitamin C punch. Oranges can improve your circulation, making you feel instantly energized.

1 Juice the fruit, then add the water. Pour into a glass, stir in the honey, if using, and add some crushed ice. Decorate with the extra currants.

makes 1 cup (8 fl oz)

blood orange

rose royce

4 oz freshly picked rosehips

1 cup (8 fl oz) boiling water

2 crisp red apples

to serve

rose petals

ice cubes

Wild roses provide an abundant, free supply of nutrient-rich rosehips which are packed with vitamin C, a powerful antioxidant essential for natural immunity and energy supply.

1 Blend the rosehips in a food processor until finely chopped. Pour into a small pan and add the water. Cover and simmer gently for 10 minutes, then leave to cool.

2 Juice the apples and strain the rosehip juice into the apple juice. Serve with rose petals and ice cubes.

makes 200 ml (7 fl oz)

NUTRITIONAL CONTENT: energy 40 cals I **calcium** 5 mg I **magnesium** 7 mg I **zinc** 0.1 mg I **vitamin C** 126 mg I **vitamin A** 37 mcg.

65

NUTRITIONAL CONTENT: energy 147 cals | **calcium** 71 mg | **magnesium** 39 mg | **zinc** 0.5 mg | **vitamin C** 31 mg | **vitamin A** 12 mcg.

1 large pear, preferably red

2 small (4 oz) parsnips

1-inch cube fresh ginger

½ cup (4 fl oz) sparkling water

Parsnips make a surprisingly delicious juice and mix well with fresh ginger and pears to make a drink that will provide plenty of slow-release energy.

1 Cut several long, thin slices from the pear and reserve. Roughly chop the remainder with the parsnips and ginger.

2 Push the parsnips and ginger, then the pear through the juicer. Pour over the pear slices in a tall glass and serve topped up with sparkling water.

makes 1 cup (8 fl oz)

energy fizz

star burst

3 whole star anise

½ teaspoon honey

¾ cup (6 fl oz) water

⅛ cantaloupe

2 mandarins or 1 small orange, peeled

Star anise has both medicinal and cosmetic uses. Its distinctive aniseed flavor blends well with melon and mandarin juice to make this refreshing, aromatic infusion with a slightly exotic touch.

1 Put the star anise and honey in a small pan with the water and bring to a slow boil. Cover and simmer very gently for 5 minutes.

2 Cut a long wedge from the melon and reserve. Cut away the rind from the remainder and roughly chop the flesh, along with the mandarins or orange.

3 Juice the fruits and mix with the strained anise syrup in a glass. Serve warm or chilled, decorated with the melon wedge.

makes 1 cup (8 fl oz)

NUTRITIONAL CONTENT: energy 103 cals I **calcium** 100 mg I **magnesium** 32 mg I **zinc** 0.3 mg I **vitamin C** 104 mg I **vitamin A** 256 mcg.

warm and spicy

1⅓ cups (8 oz) sweet green grapes

1 cinnamon stick

several lemon balm sprigs

When you need a hot drink, try this comforting treat instead of tea or coffee. Full of natural sweetness, it'll maintain your energy levels during a busy day, bringing with it the warm spiciness of cinnamon and fresh tang of lemon balm.

1 Juice the grapes and put the juice in a small pan with the cinnamon and most of the lemon balm. Heat without boiling and simmer gently, covered, for 4–5 minutes.

2 Lift out the lemon balm with a fork and pour the juice into a cup or glass. Serve decorated with the reserved lemon balm.

makes 1 cup (8 fl oz)

NUTRITIONAL CONTENT: energy 156 cals I **calcium** 63 mg I **magnesium** 26 mg I **zinc** 0.3 mg I **vitamin C** 8 mg I **vitamin A** 18 mcg.

berry mull

1 vanilla bean pod

½ teaspoon honey

½ cup (4 oz) water

⅔ pint (8 oz) strawberries

1 cup (5 oz) blueberries

small handful of raspberries, to decorate

Strawberries, raspberries and blueberries are packed with vitamins and minerals which help maintain good health and vitality, naturally. The vanilla infusion adds a subtle spiciness.

1 Split the vanilla pod with a knife and put in a small pan with the honey and water. Cover and simmer gently for 5 minutes then lift out the vanilla pod.

2 Juice the strawberries and blueberries. Add the juice to the pan and heat through gently. Pour over the raspberries in a large glass. Serve with a spoon, if desired.

makes 1 cup (8 fl oz)

NUTRITIONAL CONTENT: energy 137 cals | **calcium** 68 mg | **magnesium** 40 mg | **zinc** 0.7 mg | **vitamin C** 230 mg | **vitamin A** 11 mcg.

73

lentil power

3 tablespoons vegetable oil

2 large onions, roughly chopped

4 garlic cloves, crushed

4 teaspoons cumin seeds

1 lb dried green or brown lentils, rinsed

1 bay leaf

½ teaspoon dried oregano

10 cups (80 fl oz) chicken stock

to garnish

¾ cup sour cream

roasted cumin seeds

Lentils are an excellent source of minerals for nearly every organ in the body. They are especially effective when you are suffering from muscular fatigue as they neutralize the excess acids produced by weary muscles.

1 Heat 2 tablespoons of the oil in a saucepan and sauté the onion, garlic and 3 teaspoons of the cumin seeds for about 5 minutes, letting the onion brown and the cumin roast slightly. Add the lentils, bay leaf, oregano and stock. Bring to a boil and simmer for about 35 minutes, or until the lentils are soft.

2 Remove the bay leaf, and purée the soup in a food processor. Blend all of the soup if you like a smooth texture, or if you prefer your soups a little chunkier, blend only half of it then stir this back into the unblended part.

3 Heat the remaining oil in a small pan and sauté the remaining cumin seeds over medium heat for about 1 minute, or until they are slightly crisp. Drain on paper towels. Serve the soup in warmed bowls garnished with a tablespoon of sour cream swirled on top and the roasted cumin seeds sprinkled on top.

serves 10

NUTRITIONAL CONTENT: energy 233 cals | **protein** 14 mg | **fat** 8 mg | **carbohydrate** 29 mg | **calcium** 73 mg | **iron** 6 mg | **vitamin C** 3 mg.

76

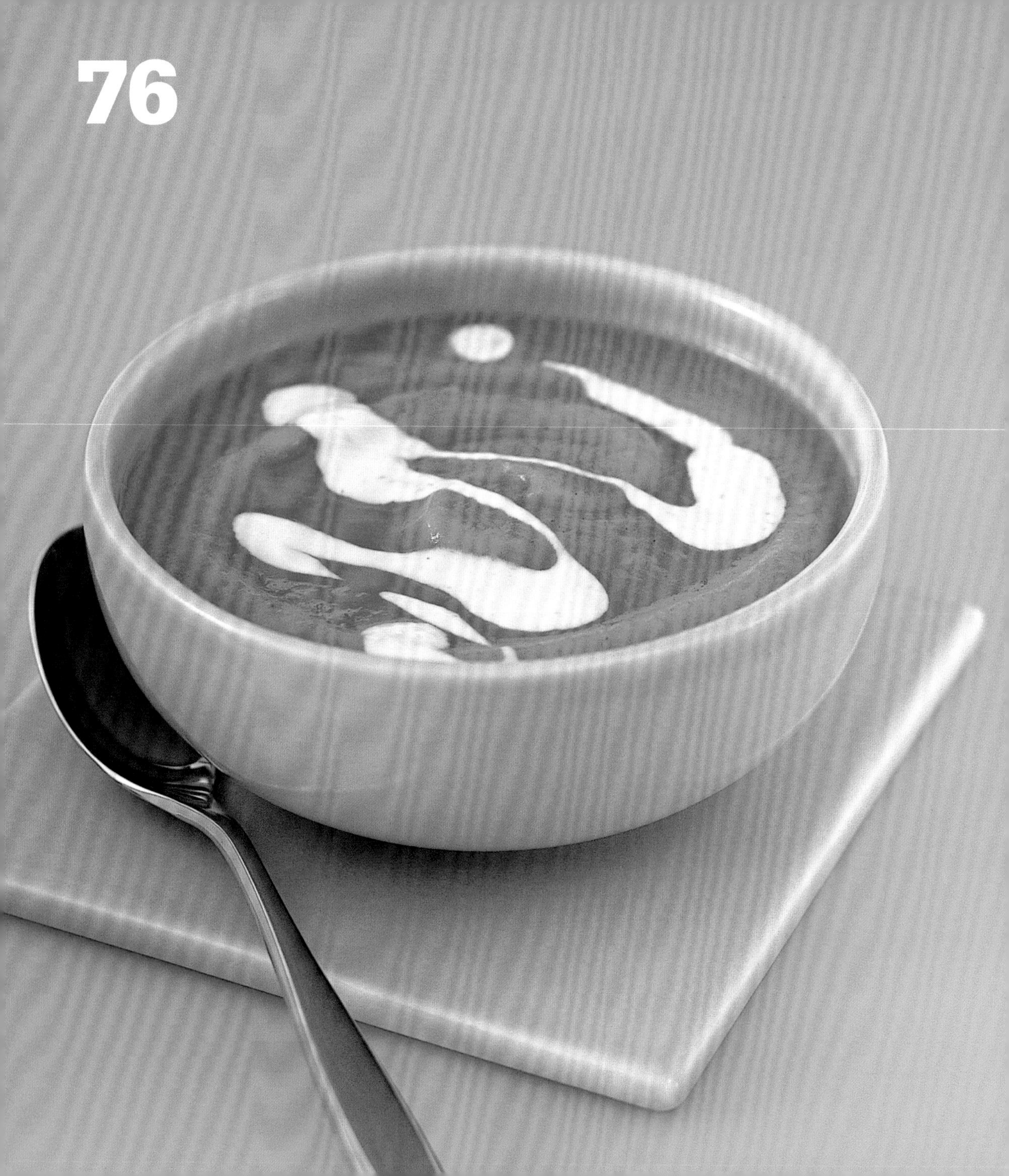

NUTRITIONAL CONTENT: energy 284 cals | protein 4 mg | fat 17 mg | carbohydrate 32 mg | calcium 49 mg | iron 2.4 mg | vitamin C 33 mg.

1 tablespoon olive oil

1 onion, roughly chopped

2 garlic cloves, crushed

1 teaspoon finely grated fresh ginger

1 teaspoon medium curry powder

1 lb sweet potato, peeled and diced

4 cups (32 fl oz) vegetable or chicken stock

salt and pepper

coconut and lime cream

½ cup (4 fl oz) coconut cream

juice of ½ lime

1 teaspoon grated lime rind

Sweet potato is the richest low-fat source of vitamin E, which is vital for energy production and cellular respiration. It contributes to heart health and is a good source of dietary antioxidants, particularly beta-carotene. It can help to lower high blood pressure and also helps anemia. It may also protect against inflammatory conditions and is attributed with anti-aging properties.

1 Heat the oil in a large saucepan over a medium heat and sauté the onion, garlic, ginger and curry powder until the onion is translucent. Add the sweet potato and cook for 1–2 minutes without browning it.

2 Add the stock, cover and cook for 10 minutes, or until the sweet potato is tender. Purée the soup in a food processor then return it to the pan and gently reheat. Season to taste.

3 To make the coconut and lime cream, mix together the coconut cream, lime juice and lime rind. Ladle the soup into bowls and garnish with a generous drizzle of the cream.

serves 4

caribbean spice

black-eyed pea bonanza

½ lb (8 oz) dried black-eyed peas, soaked in water overnight

3 tablespoons olive oil

1 onion, finely chopped

1 garlic clove, crushed

7 cups (56 fl oz) vegetable stock

1 celery stalk, sliced

1 large carrot, sliced

2 thyme sprigs

2 bay leaves

a pinch each of ground cloves and mace

salt and pepper

to garnish

2 chilies, deseeded and finely diced

1 tablespoon chopped cilantro leaves

This robust soup is packed with fiber and is very good for cleansing the digestive tract. Black-eyed peas are excellent for sustained energy and have a cholesterol-lowering effect on the bloodstream.

1 Drain and rinse the peas three times and allow to dry. Put the olive oil, onion and garlic in a large saucepan and sauté gently, covered, for about 5 minutes.

2 Add the peas and stock and bring to a boil then reduce the heat to a simmer. Add the celery, carrot, thyme, bay leaves, cloves and mace and cook for 1½ hours, or until the peas are soft.

3 Let the mixture cool slightly, discard the herbs, then purée in a food processor or blender until smooth. Return the soup to the pan and reheat it, then season with salt and pepper. Serve in warm bowls with a sprinkling of chilies and cilantro.

serves 6

NUTRITIONAL CONTENT: energy 192 cals | **protein** 9 mg | **fat** 8 mg | **carbohydrate** 22 mg | **calcium** 50 mg | **iron** 3 mg | **vitamin c** 8 mg.

79

hot stuff

2 medium (10 oz) tomatoes

2 medium (3½ oz) celery stalks, plus slivers to decorate

1-inch cube of fresh ginger, roughly chopped

1 garlic clove

1-inch cube of fresh horseradish

3 small (6 oz) carrots

ice cubes

This juice is good for bronchitis. Tomatoes and carrots provide large amounts of vitamin C, while garlic, ginger and horseradish are all-powerful antioxidants—imperative for fighting off infections. Combined, they also deal a mighty anti-mucus punch.

1 Juice all the ingredients, blend with 2 ice cubes and serve in a tumbler. Decorate with celery slivers.

makes ¾ cup (6 oz)

NUTRITIONAL CONTENT: **energy** 130 cals | **calcium** 119 mg | **magnesium** 36 mg | **zinc** 0.8 mg | **vitamin C** 32 mg | **vitamin A** 2696 mcg.

81

belly berry

2 small (8 oz) apples

1 cup (4 oz) blueberries, fresh or frozen

Apples and blueberries are both great for settling upset stomachs and combatting digestive disorders.

1 Juice the apples, then process in a blender or food processor with the blueberries. Serve in a tumbler over ice, if desired and with a straw.

makes ¾ pint (6 fl oz)

NUTRITIONAL CONTENT: energy 166 cals | calcium 26 mg | magnesium 19 mg | zinc 0.5 mg | vitamin C 36 mg | vitamin A 14 mcg.

83

NUTRITIONAL CONTENT: **energy** 171 cals | **calcium** 260 mg | **magnesium** 92 mg | **zinc** 1.3 mg | **vitamin C** 48 mg | **vitamin A** 760 mcg.

2 small (8 oz) pears, plus slices to decorate

4 (1 oz) pitted dried plums

4 oz spinach

ice cubes

This combination of fruits and vegetables is rich in fiber, with good cleansing properties to stimulate the abdomen and improve digestion. This juice really could be called a lethal weapon—a dose of three potent laxatives to relieve constipation.

1 Juice all the ingredients together and serve in a glass over ice cubes. Decorate with the extra pear slices and serve with a stirrer.

makes 1 cupl (8 fl oz)

way to go

lounge lizard

3 (8 oz) kiwis

½ small (4 oz) cucumber

1 tablespoon pomegranate seeds (if available)

slices of lime, to decorate

The vitamin C- and potassium-rich ingredients in this juice help to lower blood pressure.

1 Wash the kiwis and cucumber but do not peel them.

2 Juice both and serve with slices of lime. Stir in a tablespoon of pomegranate seeds, if available.

makes ¾ cup (6 fl oz)

NUTRITIONAL CONTENT: **energy** 143 cals | **calcium** 37 mg | **magnesium** 49 mg | **zinc** 0.4 mg | **vitamin C** 162 mg | **vitamin A** 29 mcg.

87

twister

½ medium (4 oz) pink grapefruit, plus slices to decorate

2 small (4 oz) carrots

¼ lb (4 oz) spinach

ice cubes

This juice is beneficial to arthritis sufferers. The salicylic acid in grapefruit works to break down uric acid deposits, and the carrot and spinach help to rebuild and regenerate cartilage and joints.

1 Peel the grapefruit, keeping as much of the pith as possible. Juice all the ingredients and serve over ice in a tumbler. Decorate with slices of grapefruit.

makes 1 cup (8 fl oz)

NUTRITIONAL CONTENT: energy 106 cals I **calcium** 284 mg I **magnesium** 90 mg I **zinc** 1.1 mg I **vitamin C** 83 mg I **vitamin A** 1860 mcg.

89

hula kula

½ **pineapple, peeled and roughly chopped**

½ **cup (4 fl oz) coconut milk**

½ **cup (4 fl oz) soy milk**

pineapple leaf, to decorate

A tropical smoothie that uses pineapple to aid digestion. Choose a soy milk enriched with calcium and vitamins to make the nutritional content even better.

1 Place all the ingredients in a blender with some ice cubes and blend until the mixture is smooth. Decorate with pineapple leaves.

makes 1 cup (8 fl oz)

NUTRITIONAL CONTENT: energy 142 cals I **calcium** 80 mg I **magnesium** 79 mg I **zinc** 0.5 mg I **vitamin C** 28 mg I **vitamin A** 6 mcg.

91

sweet chariot

¼ **pineapple, peeled and roughly chopped**

½ **cup (3½ oz) grapes**

1 small orange, plus wedges to decorate

1 small apple

½ **large mango, peeled**

½ **large banana, peeled**

ice cubes

mint leaves, cut into strips, to decorate

A mini-meal in a glass, this smoothie is high in calcium, magnesium and phosphorus, all essential for protecting bones and maintaining body cells. There's also a high vitamin C content, for fighting infection and viruses.

1 Juice the pineapple, grapes, orange and apple. Process in a blender with the mango, banana and a couple of ice cubes. Serve decorated with orange wedges and strips of mint.

makes about 2 cups (14 fl oz)

NUTRITIONAL CONTENT: energy 227 cals | **calcium** 103 mg | **magnesium** 69 mg | **zinc** 0.6 mg | **vitamin C** 118 mg | **vitamin A** 241 mcg.

93

passion thriller

½ **honeydew melon, rind removed**

½ **small (4 oz) cucumber**

1 **small avocado, peeled and pitted**

¼ **cup (2 oz) dried apricots, plus slivers to decorate**

1 **tablespoon wheat germ**

ice cubes

A cool-looking smoothie high in vitamin E (great for smooth skin). It also contains selenium, an essential trace mineral for blood formation.

1 Juice the melon and cucumber. Process in a blender with the avocado, apricots, wheat germ and a couple of ice cubes. Decorate with dried apricot slivers.

makes 1 cup (8 fl oz)

NUTRITIONAL CONTENT: energy 343 cals I **calcium** 98 mg I **magnesium** 96 mg I **zinc** 1.9 mg I **vitamin C** 27 mg I **vitamin A** 68 mcg.

95

acher shaker

⅓ pint (4 oz) strawberries, hulled

½ pineapple, plus wedges to decorate

1 banana, peeled

ice cubes

Plenty of fruits and vegetables can help keep arthritic pains at bay. The high vitamin C content of this drink makes it a great pick-me-up.

1 Juice the strawberries and pineapple. Pour the juice into a blender, add the banana and a couple of ice cubes and process. Serve with a spoon and decorated with a couple of pineapple wedges and a stirrer.

makes 1 cup (6 fl oz)

NUTRITIONAL CONTENT: energy 206 cals **ı calcium** 66 mg **ı magnesium** 77 mg **ı zinc** 0.5 mg **ı vitamin C** 116 mg **ı vitamin A** 12 mcg.

NUTRITIONAL CONTENT: energy 173 cals | calcium 211 mg | magnesium 90 mg | zinc 0.8 mg | vitamin C 140 mg | vitamin A 86 mcg.

2 grapefruit

1½ lbs cucumber, plus slices to decorate

1 lemon, plus slices to decorate

sparkling mineral water

mint leaves, to decorate

ice cubes

A cooling drink to savor on a hot day. Like most citrus fruits, grapefruit is a good source of calcium, essential for the maintenance of strong bones, as well as being rich in vitamin C.

1 Juice the grapefruit, cucumber and lemon. Pour into a jug over ice, and top up with sparkling mineral water to make up to 2 cups (14 fl oz). Decorate with mint leaves and slices of cucumber and lemon.

makes about 2 cups (14 fl oz)

karma kooler

zesty ginger beer

1 oz fresh ginger

1 lime

boiling water

2 tablespoons honey

¾ cup sparkling water

Ginger is one of the best healing foods available, great for relieving upset stomachs, indigestion and nausea and for clearing the sinuses. It also gets the circulation going and soothes the pain of arthritis, so it's definitely an ingredient worth some space in the refrigerator.

1 Finely grate the ginger into a measuring jug, then scrape the pulp left on the grater into the jug. Grate the lime rind and add to the ginger. Make up to ½ cup (4 fl oz) with boiling water and let stand for 10 minutes.

2 Strain into a tall glass and stir in the honey and squeeze in the lime juice. Chill the juice if you like an ice cold drink and serve topped up with sparkling water.

makes 1 cup (8 fl oz)

NUTRITIONAL CONTENT: energy 158 cals I **calcium** 10 mg I **magnesium** 3 mg I **zinc** 0.5 mg I **vitamin C** 12 mg I **vitamin A** 3 mcg.

101

102

NUTRITIONAL CONTENT: energy 137 cals I **calcium** 60 mg I **magnesium** 29 mg I **zinc** 1 mg I **vitamin C** 14 mg I **vitamin A** 29 mcg.

2 small (3½ oz) beets

½ small fennel bulb

¾ cup (5 oz) black or red grapes

crushed ice

These vegetables are a real powerhouse of goodness, brilliant as a general pick-me-up if you're feeling lethargic, dehydrated or simply hungover. Juiced beets are surprisingly sweet so you might want to add a squeeze of lemon juice as well.

1 Roughly chop the beets and fennel and push through the juicer along with the grapes. Pour over crushed ice in a tall glass and serve immediately.

makes 1 cup (8 fl oz)

beet this

tummy tonic

5 cardamom pods

good pinch of cumin seeds

3 mint sprigs, plus extra leaves, to decorate

1 green tea bag

1 cup (8 fl oz) boiling water

honey, to taste

Mint is a vital ingredient in natural remedies, particularly as an aid to digestion. Cardamom pods are also good for the digestive system and, along with the cumin, turn this into a deliciously spicy, aromatic blend.

1 Lightly crush the cardamon pods and cumin seeds using a mortar and pestle. Add the mint sprigs and bruise the leaves to release the flavor. Turn them into a small jug or teapot along with the teabag and make up to 1 cup (8 fl oz) with the boiling water.

2 Let infuse for 4 minutes then strain into a cup. Add a little honey to taste and serve decorated with extra mint leaves.

makes 1 cup (8 fl oz)

NUTRITIONAL CONTENT: energy 24 cals | **calcium** 36 mg | **magnesium** 11 mg | **zinc** 0.2 mg | **vitamin C** 1 mg | **vitamin A** 6 mcg.

105

fever fusion

4 large feverfew sprigs

3–4 fresh or dried hibiscus flowers

pared strip of lemon rind

1 cup (8 fl oz) boiling water

1 teaspoon lemon juice

honey, to taste

Feverfew is renowned as a cure for headaches and fever, hence its name. In herbal medicine it's still widely used as a treatment for migraines because of its ability to improve blood vessel functioning and reduce inflammation. Both flowers and leaves can be used.

1 Put 3 of the feverfew sprigs, the hibiscus and lemon rind in a cup and add the boiling water. Leave to infuse for 4–5 minutes. Lift out the herbs and lemon rind and stir in the lemon juice and a little honey, to taste. Decorate with the remaining sprig of feverfew.

makes 1 cup (8 fl oz)

NUTRITIONAL CONTENT: energy 14 cals | **calcium** 7 mg | **magnesium** 3 mg | **zinc** trace | **vitamin C** 4 mg | **vitamin A** 0 mcg.

107

c for comfort

1 cup (5 oz) currants

3 thyme sprigs

1 cup (8 fl oz) boiling water

honey, to taste

Sore throats and coughs can really benefit from a dose of this comforting tea. Currants are rich in vitamin C and give a vital boost to the body's own natural defences. Fresh thyme has antiseptic properties and, combined with the honey, eases any discomfort.

1 Pour the currants into a bowl and add the thyme and boiling water. Using a fork, mash the currants against the side of the bowl to release all the juices.

2 Leave for 2 minutes then strain into a warmed cup. Add a little honey to taste.

makes 1 cup (8 fl oz)

NUTRITIONAL CONTENT: energy 54 cals | **calcium** 90 mg | **magnesium** 26 mg | **zinc** 0.5 mg | **vitamin C** 300 mg | **vitamin A** 25 mcg.

109

NUTRITIONAL CONTENT: **energy** 250 cals | **protein** 29 g | **fat** 12 g | **carbohydrate** 7 g | **calcium** 330 mg | **iron** 3 mg | **vitamin C** 24 mg.

1 lb asparagus

2 tablespoons olive oil

2 medium (4 oz) celery stalks, sliced

2 (4 oz) leeks, sliced

½ medium (4 oz) onion, sliced

5 cups (40 fl oz) chicken stock

7 oz silken tofu

1 cup (10 oz) cooked chicken, cut into bite-sized pieces

1 teaspoon chopped thyme

salt and pepper

2 tablespoons chopped tarragon, to garnish

This soup is high in protein, low in carbohydrates and contains only healthy fat. It is an excellent choice for a low carbohydrate diet. If you are recovering from an illness the powerful combination of healthy protein and calcium will aid a speedy recovery.

1 Trim the bottoms of the asparagus stalks where they begin to turn white. Cut off the tips about 1½ inches from the top and set aside. Roughly slice the remaining sections.

2 Heat the oil in a large saucepan, add the celery, leeks and onions and fry until soft. Add the stock and bring to the boil. Add the sliced asparagus and simmer for 5 minutes. Remove the soup from the heat and blend in a food processor with the tofu.

3 Return the soup to the pan and season with salt and pepper. Add the asparagus tips, chicken pieces and thyme and simmer for 10 minutes. Pour into warm serving bowls and sprinkle with chopped tarragon.

serves 4

recovery

chill-out

1 garlic bulb, skin left on

1 cup (4 oz) fresh white breadcrumbs

4 cups (32 fl oz) chicken or vegetable stock

¾ cup (4 oz) blanched almonds, lightly toasted

5 tablespoons olive oil

1½ tablespoons red wine vinegar

salt and pepper

to garnish

2 oranges, segmented

halved black and green grapes

toasted almonds

handful of cilantro and mint leaves

Almonds contain phosphorus and magnesium, both crucial for strong bones, so this soup can reduce the risk or effects of osteoporosis. Nuts are also known to reduce levels of LDL (bad cholesterol). Garlic is a powerful blood thinner and general circulatory tonic.

1 Roast the garlic bulb in a preheated oven at 350°F (180°C), for about 30 minutes until soft. Meanwhile, soak the breadcrumbs in 150 ml (¼ pint) of the stock for 5 minutes.

2 Remove the garlic from the oven and let it cool, then squeeze the pulp into the bread mixture. Blend the almonds in a food processor until finely ground. Add the bread mixture to the almonds and blend. Gradually add the oil until it forms a smooth paste, then add the remainder of the stock and the sherry vinegar and process until smooth.

3 Transfer the soup to a bowl and season with salt and pepper. Cover and chill for at least 2–3 hours. Serve the soup in chilled bowls garnished with orange segments, grapes, toasted almonds, cilantro and mint.

serves 6

NUTRITIONAL CONTENT: energy 287 cals I **protein** 7 g I **fat** 22 g I **carbohydrate** 17 g I **calcium** 96 mg I **iron** 1.2 mg I **vitamin C** 23 mg.

fiery indian broth

¼ cup (½ stick) butter

1 large onion, chopped

3 garlic cloves, chopped

1 teaspoon cumin seeds

1 teaspoon ground coriander

pinch of ground cinnamon

pinch of ground nutmeg

1 teaspoon chopped fresh ginger

½ teaspoon ground cloves

1 red chili, seeded and finely chopped

½ teaspoon ground cardamom

8 oz dried green lentils

5 cups (40 fl oz) vegetable stock

1 lb spinach

1 cup (8 oz) Greek yogurt

salt and pepper

The staples of Indian cuisine are recommended by health professionals to prevent heart disease, obesity, cancer, diabetes and stroke. Lentils are little vitamin pills—full of B vitamins—and good for energy production. Dry skin benefits from the vitamin B2 in both the lentils and yogurt, which is also good for digestion.

1 Melt the butter in a large heavy saucepan, add the onion, garlic, cumin, coriander, cinnamon, nutmeg, ginger, cloves, chili and cardamom and fry for 5 minutes.

2 Add the lentils and stir for about 2 minutes. Pour in the stock, bring to a boil and simmer, covered, for 1 hour.

3 Chop the spinach finely, add it to the broth and simmer for 5 minutes. Stir in the yogurt, season with salt and pepper and heat through gently for 1 minute. Serve the soup in warmed bowls or mugs.

serves 6

NUTRITIONAL CONTENT: energy 257 cals | **protein** 14 g | **fat** 13 g | **carbohydrate** 23 g | calcium 260 mg | iron 6.6 mg | **vitamin C** 26 mg.

115

sour power

1 pomegranate

1 carrot

½ cup (3½ oz) grapes

crushed ice

The tangy taste of pomegranate enlivens this cleansing drink, which is high in protective carotenes.

1 Scoop out the pomegranate pulp and seeds. Reserve a few seeds for decoration, then juice the pulp and the rest of the seeds with the carrot and grapes. Serve over crushed ice mixed with the reserved pomegranate seeds.

makes 1 cup (8 fl oz)

NUTRITIONAL CONTENT: energy 117 cals | **calcium** 36 mg | **magnesium** 17 mg | **zinc** 0.4 mg | **vitamin C** 16 mg | **vitamin A** 818 mcg.

117

NUTRITIONAL CONTENT: energy 86 cals | **calcium** 30 mg | **magnesium** 23 mg | **zinc** 0.2 mg | **vitamin C** 72 mg | **vitamin A** 42 mcg.

1 peach

2 plums, pitted, plus wedges to decorate

1 kiwi

ice cubes

This juice is rich in beta-carotenes from the peaches and plums, and high in potassium, which is good for regulating blood pressure. Plum juice stimulates bowel action, preventing the discomfort of constipation.

1 Juice all the ingredients together and serve over ice cubes. Decorate with plum wedges.

makes 1 cup (8 fl oz)

plum punch

purple passion

2 cups (8 oz) blueberries

½ grapefruit

2 large apples

1-inch cube of fresh ginger, plus thin strips to decorate

The combination of these three fruits, plus the zest of ginger, makes this a great drink for clearing the system and warding off infection.

1 Juice all the ingredients together and serve in a tall glass with ice cubes. Decorate with thin strips of ginger.

makes 1 cup (8 fl oz)

NUTRITIONAL CONTENT: energy 247 cals | **calcium** 63 mg | **magnesium** 35 mg | **zinc** 0.8 mg | **vitamin C** 90 mg | **vitamin A** 25 mcg.

bumpy ride

**2 small apples, plus slices
to decorate**

1 small beet

2 celery sticks

ice cubes

Beets are rich in folate, important for blood and for the nervous system. The high fluid content is ideal for first thing in the morning.

1 Juice all the ingredients together and serve in a tumbler over ice. Decorate with apple slices and serve with a straw.

makes ¾ cup (6 fl oz)

NUTRITIONAL CONTENT: energy 85 cals | **calcium** 40 mg | **magnesium** 15 mg | **zinc** 0.4 mg | **vitamin C** 15 mg | **vitamin A** 11 mcg.

123

papaya flyer

**½ large pear, plus slices
to decorate**

1 carrot

¼ papaya, peeled and seeded

1 ice cube

This delicious juice is rich in vitamin C and beta-carotene.
The natural sweetness of pear, carrot and papaya will give an
instant energy kick first thing in the morning, or indeed at any
time of the day.

1 Juice the pear and carrot and put in a blender with the
papaya and an ice cube and blend until smooth. Decorate
with thin slices of pear.

makes 1 cup (8 fl oz)

NUTRITIONAL CONTENT: energy 145 cals I **calcium** 70 mg I **magnesium** 23 mg I **zinc** 0.8 mg I
vitamin C 115 mg I **vitamin A** 1386 mcg.

125

126

NUTRITIONAL CONTENT: energy 128 cals I calcium 66 mg I magnesium 61 mg I zinc 1.3 mg I vitamin C 18 mg I vitamin A 21 mcg.

¼ **pineapple**

1 small apple

4 oz alfalfa sprouts

4 fl oz soy milk

ice cubes

Alfalfa sprouts contain folate, magnesium, zinc and phosphorus, all essential for the formation, repair and healing of body tissue. This is a great all-around drink.

1 Juice the pineapple, apple and alfalfa sprouts together. Pour the juice into a blender with the soy milk and an ice cube and blend. Serve over ice cubes with a straw.

makes 1 cup (8 fl oz)

full tank

berry nice

2 bananas, peeled

¾ pint (7 oz) raspberries, plus extra to decorate

¾ cup (4 oz) blueberries, plus extra to decorate

1 small glass of unsweetened cranberry juice

2 tablespoons live yogurt

Packed with energy and vitamin C, as well as calcium and magnesium which are necessary for cell repair, this colorful smoothie makes a tangy and healthy start to anyone's day.

1 Roughly chop the bananas and put into a blender. Add the berries and pour in the cranberry juice. Add the yogurt and blend until smooth. Pour into a glass and decorate with the extra blueberries and raspberries.

makes 1 cup (8 fl oz)

NUTRITIONAL CONTENT: energy 333 cals I **calcium** 227 mg I **magnesium** 114 mg I **zinc** 1.7 mg I **vitamin C** 134 mg I **vitamin A** 21 mcg.

green dream

2 large apples

1 celery stick

½ kiwi, plus a slice to decorate

½ lemon

1 small avocado

This smoothie is refreshing, cleansing and instantly invigorating, with a high vitamin E content to promote lovely smooth skin.

1 Juice the apple, celery, kiwi and lemon. Transfer to a blender and process with the avocado for 20 seconds to make a refreshing smoothie. Decorate with kiwi slices.

makes 1 cup (8 fl oz)

NUTRITIONAL CONTENT: energy 352 cals | **calcium** 45 mg | **magnesium** 48 mg | **zinc** 0.8 mg | **vitamin C** 53 mg | **vitamin A** 17 mcg.

131

NUTRITIONAL CONTENT: **energy** 311 cals | **calcium** 263 mg | **magnesium** 64 mg | **zinc** 2.1 mg | **vitamin C** 22 mg | **vitamin A** 13 mcg.

½ cup (2 oz) shelled pecans

1 cup (8 oz) live yogurt

1 cup (8 fl oz) apple juice

honey, to taste

ice cubes

Rich in calcium and magnesium for the protection of bone and cell tissue, this drink also contains pecans and is packed with protein to set you up for the day.

1 Put the pecans into a food processor or blender with a few tablespoons of the yogurt and process to a paste.

2 Add the remaining yogurt and the apple juice and process again until well mixed. Sweeten to taste with honey and serve over ice.

makes 2 heaping cups (18 fl oz)

pecan punch

fruity filler

6 dried apricots

½ cup (2 oz) raisins

¼ cup (1 oz) shelled pistachios

1 cup (8 fl oz) coconut milk

1 cup (8 fl oz) apricot juice

sugar, to taste

ice cubes

Apricots and raisins are rich in potassium, good for blood pressure control, and pistachios provide selenium, which is good for the blood. Altogether a power-packed smoothie, this drink is great as an occasional meal replacement.

1 Place the dried apricots, raisins and pistachios in a food processor or blender with a little of the coconut milk and process for 1 minute to make a smooth paste.

2 Add the remaining coconut milk and the apricot juice and process until will mixed. Add sugar to taste, drizzle a little coconut milk over the top and serve over ice.

makes 2 heaping cups (18 fl oz)

NUTRITIONAL CONTENT: **energy** 555 cals | **calcium** 153 mg | **magnesium** 108 mg | **zinc** 0.7 mg | **vitamin C** 65 mg | **vitamin A** 56 mcg.

135

cool and cleansing

1 large apple

¼ pint (3 oz) blackberries

¾ cup (6 fl oz) water

ice cubes

Keep some blackberries in the freezer to make this cleansing drink in winter or summer. It tastes good and provides vitamins C and E.

1 Juice the apple and blackberries together then stir in the water. Pour into a glass and add a couple of ice cubes to chill. Serve with a stirrer.

makes 1 cup (8 fl oz)

NUTRITIONAL CONTENT: **energy** 66 cals I **calcium** 35 mg I **magnesium** 22 mg I **zinc** 0.3 mg I **vitamin C** 17 mg I **vitamin A** 13 mcg.

tropicana

1 small ripe mango

2 passion fruits

juice of 1 lime

½ cup (4 fl oz) live yogurt

ice cubes

Mango is packed with vitamin C and beta-carotene and provides a good dose of slow-release energy. A ripe mango blends to a deliciously thick consistency and is perfect for a breakfast substitute.

1 Halve the mango. Scoop all the flesh into a blender, discarding the peel and pit. Halve the passion fruits and scoop the pulp into the blender.

2 Add the lime juice and yogurt and blend until smooth, scraping the mixture down from the sides of the blender if necessary. Pour over crushed ice in a tall glass.

makes 1 cup (8 fl oz)

NUTRITIONAL CONTENT: **energy** 155 cals | **calcium** 214 mg | **magnesium** 49 mg | **zinc** 1 mg | **vitamin C** 73 mg | **vitamin A** 497 mcg.

139

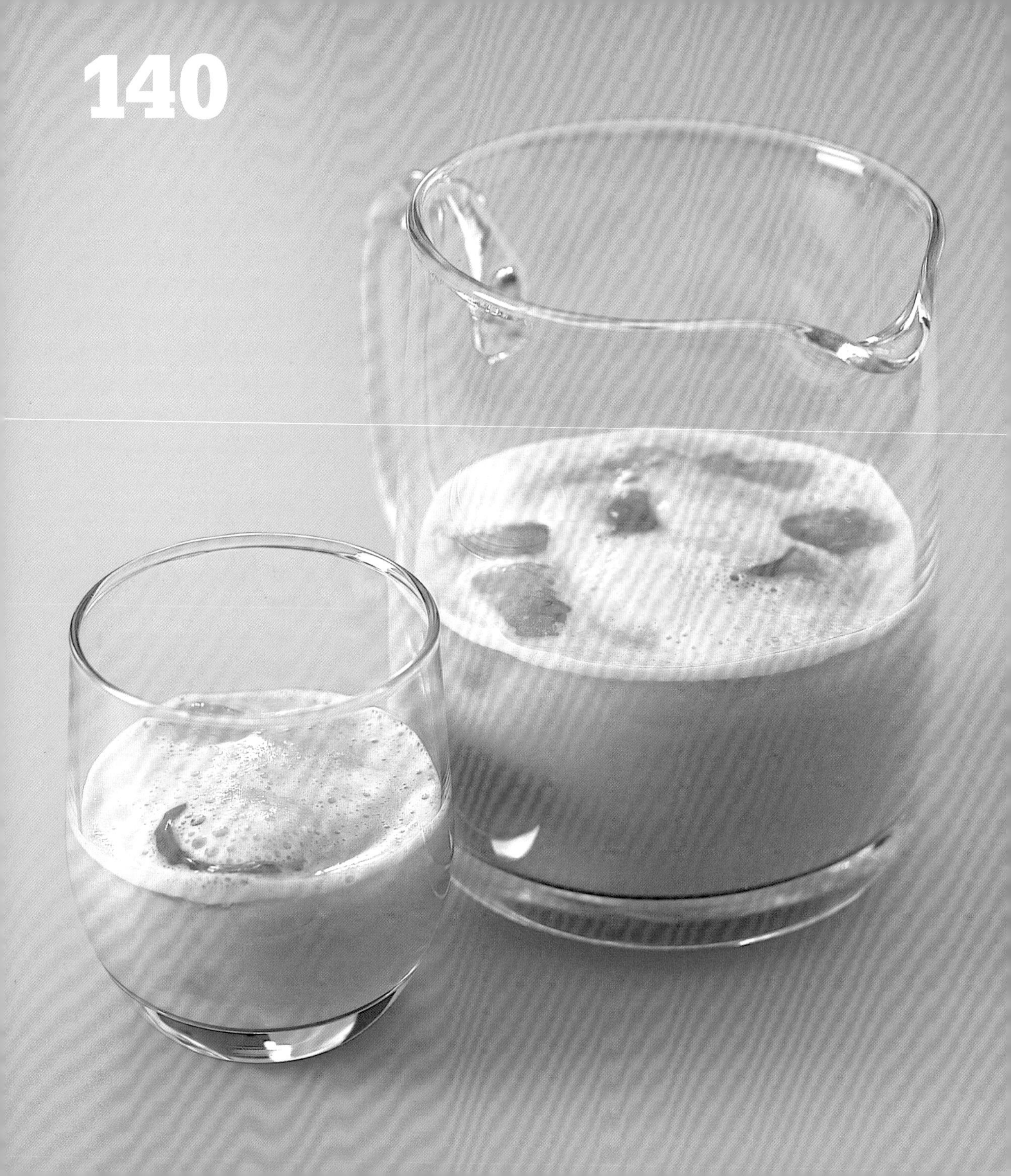

NUTRITIONAL CONTENT: **energy** 209 cals I **calcium** 105 mg I **magnesium** 42 mg I **zinc** 0.6 mg I **vitamin C** 148 mg I **vitamin A** 13 mcg.

1 pomelo

1 red grapefruit

½ cup (4 fl oz) soy milk

2–3 teaspoons honey

ice cubes

This frothy pink cooler is light on calories and packed with invigorating nutrients. Sweet pomelo and red grapefruit go together to make an interesting drink but you could use two yellow grapefruits instead.

1 First squeeze the juice from the pomelo and grapefruit. To extract maximum juice from large citrus fruits, cut away the thick skins, chop the flesh and push it through a juicer.

2 Mix the juice in a bowl with the soy milk and honey. Blend with an electric whisk until a thick froth forms on the surface. Pour into a glass and serve with ice cubes.

makes 1 cup (8 fl oz)

citrus squeeze

ginger spice

4 medium (10 oz) carrots

¼ cup (2 oz) fennel, plus strips and fronds, to serve

2 medium (3 oz) celery stalks

1-inch cube fresh ginger, roughly chopped

1 tablespoon spirulina (optional)

ice cubes

Drink a glass of this juice before a light lunch to give you an instant energy boost and banish the dieting blues.

1 Juice the ingredients and serve over ice, with fennel fronds mixed in. You can also add 1 tablespoon of spirulina, which contains phenylalanine, to fill you up. If desired, decorate with strips of fennel.

makes 1 cup (8 fl oz)

NUTRITIONAL CONTENT: **energy** 183 cals | **potassium** 1627 mg | **magnesium** 80 mg | **vitamin C** 43 mg | **vitamin A** 25,380 mcg.

tongue tingler

**3 mint sprigs, plus extra,
to decorate**

½ orange

1 cup (8 fl oz) boiling water

1 passion fruit

1–2 teaspoons honey

An infusion releases a burst of flavor from even the smallest sprig of mint. Mixed with vitamin-packed orange and passion fruit, this tingling tea will get you off to a good start.

1 Crush the mint between your fingers to bruise it, then put it in a cup. Pare a strip of rind from the orange and add to the cup with the boiling water. Leave for 3–4 minutes then lift out the mint sprigs.

2 Halve the passion fruit and press the pulp through a tea strainer set over the cup to extract the juice. Squeeze the orange juice and add to the cup with honey to taste. Stir well and serve with extra mint sprigs.

makes 1 cup (8 fl oz)

NUTRITIONAL CONTENT: energy 70 cals I **calcium** 44 mg I **magnesium** 13 mg I **zinc** 0.3 mg I **vitamin C** 47 mg I **vitamin A** 25 mcg.

cleansing cranberry

1 cinnamon stick

½ oz fresh ginger, thinly sliced

½ cup (4 fl oz) water

1 cup (7 oz) fresh cranberries

1 small dessert apple, roughly chopped

3–4 teaspoons honey

Cranberries are rich in vitamin C and among the most cleansing of fruits, warding off bacteria and viruses. Tangy and refreshing, this is a great infusion to kick start the day.

1 Cut the cinnamon stick into two and set one half aside. Break the other half into small pieces and heat it together with the ginger and water in a small pan. Heat gently without boiling for 5 minutes then leave to cool.

2 Juice the cranberries and apple. Strain the liquid in the pan into the fruit juice, then return to the cleaned pan with the honey. Heat through until the honey has dissolved and pour into a cup to serve. Serve with the reserved piece of cinnamon stick as a stirrer.

makes 1 cup (8 fl oz)

NUTRITIONAL CONTENT: **energy** 103 cals I **calcium** 30 mg I **magnesium** 18 mg I **zinc** 0.6 mg I **vitamin C** 30 mg I **vitamin A** 11 mcg.

147

berried treasure

8 cloves

1 cup (8 fl oz) boiling water

⅓ pint (3½ oz) raspberries, plus extra, to decorate

1–2 teaspoons honey

Try this infusion if you need a warming boost. It is at its best when raspberries are at their sweetest and juiciest. Cloves add a warm spiciness, but don't use too many as they will overpower the fruit.

1 Put the cloves in a small bowl and add half the boiling water. Leave for 5 minutes.

2 Mash the raspberries in a separate bowl and add the remaining boiling water. Lift out the cloves from the infused water and press the raspberry pulp through a sieve into the bowl. Stir, pour into a warmed cup and stir in the honey to taste. Decorate with the extra raspberries.

makes 1 cup (8 fl oz)

NUTRITIONAL CONTENT: energy 48 cals | **calcium** 25 mg | **magnesium** 19 mg | **zinc** 0.4 mg | **vitamin C** 32 mg | **vitamin A** 1 mcg.

150

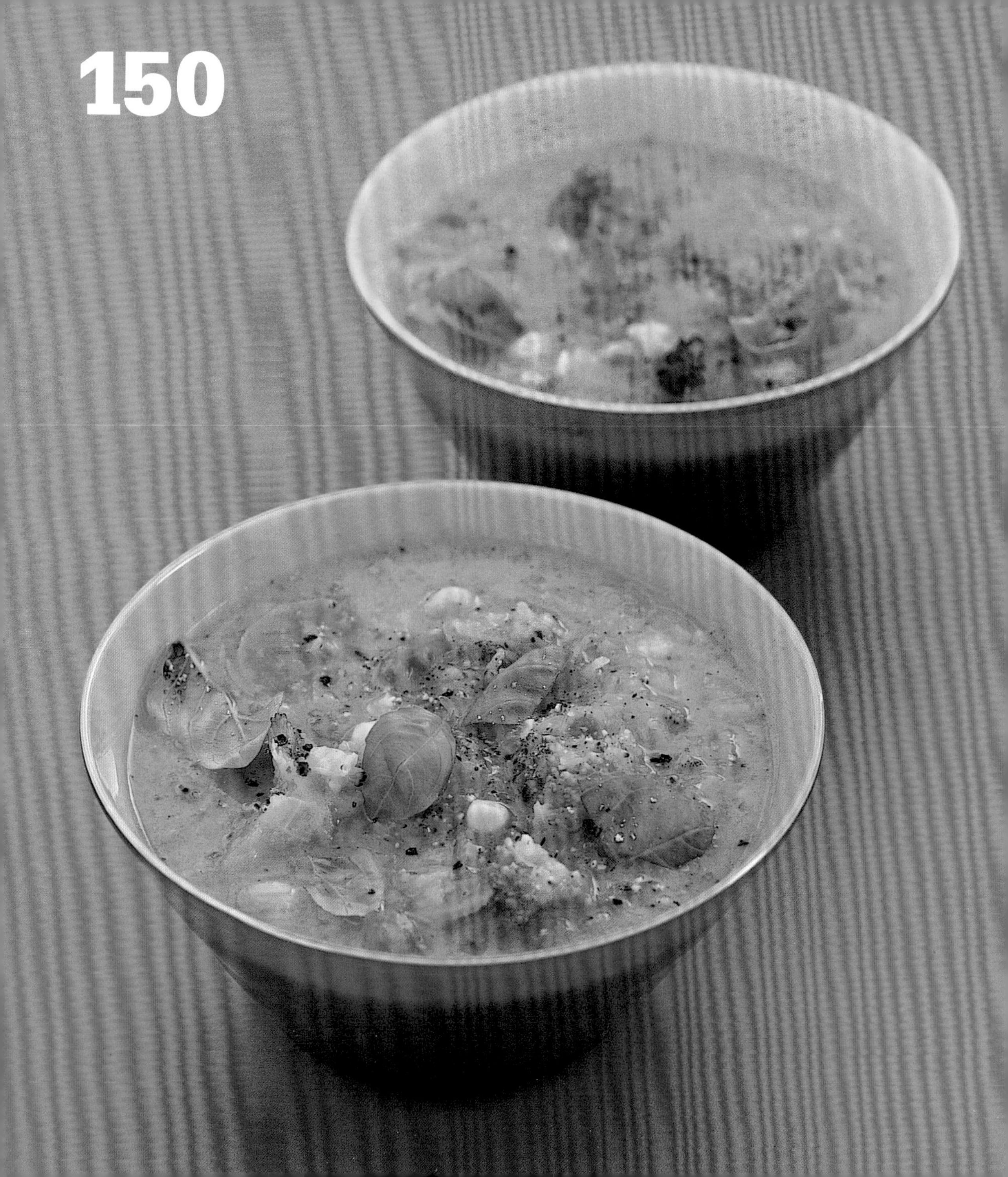

NUTRITIONAL CONTENT: energy 246 cals | protein 8 g | fat 10 g | carbohydrate 32 g | calcium 93 mg | iron 2.6 mg | vitamin C 66 mg.

1 tablespoon olive oil

2 tablespoons butter

1 onion, finely chopped

1 leek, finely chopped

1 celery stalk, finely chopped

3 garlic cloves, chopped

2 carrots, sliced

1 small (8 oz) squash, peeled and diced

1 medium (6 oz) potato, peeled and diced

4 cups (32 fl oz) vegetable stock

2 cups (6 oz) broccoli florets

¾ cup (4 oz) defrosted frozen sweet corn kernels

¾ cup (7 oz) canned tomatoes

¾ cup (6 fl oz) soy milk

salt and pepper

basil leaves, to garnish

Full of immune-boosting antioxidants, this chowder is the perfect antidote to cold winter weather. If you feel a cold on the way, add a few extra garlic cloves. Don't overcook the soup or you will destroy the nutrients.

1 Heat the oil and butter in a large heavy saucepan, add the onion, leek, celery and garlic and cook gently until softened. Add the carrots, squash and potatoes and stir for about 5 minutes. Add the stock, cover and cook for 10 minutes.

2 Add the broccoli, sweet corn and tomatoes and cook for 5 minutes. Remove from the heat and allow to cool slightly. Stir in the soy milk and season to taste.

3 Put the soup into a food processor and blend to a rough purée. Pour the soup back into the pan and gently reheat. Serve in warm bowls, scattered with basil leaves.

serves 4

chunky chowder

brain booster

2 teaspoons olive oil

1 teaspoon sesame oil

2 garlic cloves, finely chopped

1-inch piece of fresh ginger, peeled and chopped

2 green onions, finely chopped

1 red chili, seeded and finely chopped

1 lemongrass stalk

2 kaffir lime leaves

1 tablespoon lemon juice

2 teaspoons ground coriander

3 cups (24 fl oz) chicken stock

1 lb papaya, peeled, seeded and diced

8 oz silken tofu, diced

2 tablespoons coconut milk

to garnish

thin strips of red pepper

2 tablespoons cilantro leaves

This fragrant soup is a satisfying meal in a bowl. Papaya aids digestion, while tofu rebalances hormones and lowers LDL (bad cholesterol). This soup is rich in calcium, which maintains healthy bones and teeth. Vegetable stock may be used instead of chicken stock.

1 Heat the olive oil in a saucepan with the sesame oil and sauté the garlic, ginger and half the spring onion until soft. Add the chili and cook for 1 more minute. Add the lemongrass and lime leaves, the lemon juice and ground coriander. Stir in the stock and papaya and simmer for 15 minutes.

2 Strain the soup through a fine sieve into a clean saucepan. Push it through with a wooden spoon to ensure all the papaya pulp goes through.

3 Add the tofu and cook for 5 minutes, then stir in the coconut milk. Serve the soup hot or cold with the remaining spring onion, the red pepper and cilantro leaves, which should be chopped at the last minute.

serves 4

NUTRITIONAL CONTENT: energy 178 cals | **protein** 7 g | **fat** 10 g | **carbohydrate** 17 g | **calcium** 370 mg | **iron** 2.2 mg | **vitamin C** 99 mg.

evergreen

1 large (2 oz) celery stalk

¼ cup (2 oz) fennel

¼ lb (4 oz) romaine lettuce

¾ cup (6 oz) pineapple

1 teaspoon chopped tarragon, plus extra sprigs to decorate

ice cubes

This juice combines celery and fennel, which help the body to utilize magnesium, and calcium which calms the nerves. With the added sedative effect of the lettuce, this drink makes an ideal stress-buster.

1 Juice the celery, fennel, lettuce, pineapple, and chopped tarragon and chop in a blender or food processor with 2 ice cubes. Serve in a tall glass and decorate with a stirrer and tarragon sprigs.

makes 1 cup (8 fl oz)

NUTRITIONAL CONTENT: energy 101 cals I **calcium** 108 mg I **magnesium** 45 mg I **zinc** 0.8 mg I **vitamin C** 34 mg I **vitamin A** 98 mcg.

155

½ cup (4 oz) pineapple

¾ cup (4 oz) grapes

⅛ lb (2 oz) lettuce

1 large (2 oz) celery stalk

endive leaves to decorate

ice cubes

Pineapple and grapes give a boost of blood sugar, which can help to induce sleep. Lettuce and celery relax the nerves and muscles.

1 Juice all the ingredients together and serve in a tall glass over ice. Decorate with endive leaves.

makes 1 cup (8 fl oz)

sleep tight

morning after

½ **small (4 oz) papaya, plus slices to decorate**

2 oranges

½ **small (4 oz) cucumber, plus slices, to decorate**

ice cubes

Papaya helps to calm the digestive system, cucumber flushes out toxins and orange gives a great boost of vitamin C. The overall effect is calming and rehydrating.

1 Peel the papaya and the oranges, leaving as much pith on the oranges as possible. Juice them together with the cucumber and serve in a tall glass over ice. Decorate with the extra slices of cucumber and papaya.

makes 1 cup (8 fl oz)

NUTRITIONAL CONTENT: energy 187 cals I **calcium** 203 mg I **magnesium** 52 mg I **zinc** 0.9 mg I **vitamin C** 267 mg I **vitamin A** 175 mcg.

159

herbi-four

1 medium (6 oz) red pepper

1 medium (6 oz) tomato

⅛ small (3½ oz) cabbage

1 tablespoon chopped parsley

lime wedges, to decorate

ice cubes

This juice is particularly good for the skin, which, as the body's largest organ of elimination, is the barometer of health and therefore the first to show any imbalances.

1 Juice the red pepper, tomatoes and cabbage. Pour into a tall glass over ice, stir in the parsley, decorate with thin wedges of lime and serve with a straw.

makes 1 cup (8 fl oz)

NUTRITIONAL CONTENT: energy 114 cals I **calcium** 85 mg I **magnesium** 44 mg I **zinc** 0.6 mg I **vitamin C** 319 mg I **vitamin A** 1347 mcg.

161

vision impeccable

3 small (6 oz) carrots

¼ lb (4 oz) endive

2 medium (4 oz) celery stalks

to serve

lemon slices

1 teaspoon chopped parsley

Carrots contain high levels of beta-carotene and vitamin E, which are necessary for maintaining healthy eyes. Endive is helpful in preventing cataracts. This combination of vegetables provides vitamin A to nourish the optic nerve.

1 Juice the carrots, endive and celery. Process in a blender with a couple of ice cubes and serve with lemon slices and chopped parsley stirred in.

makes 1 cup (8 fl oz)

NUTRITIONAL CONTENT: energy 78 cals I **calcium** 166 mg I **magnesium** 35 mg I **zinc** 0.7 mg I **vitamin C** 32 mg I **vitamin A** 1656 mcg.

163

NUTRITIONAL CONTENT: **energy** 303 cals I **calcium** 132 mg I **magnesium** 126 mg I **zinc** 1.4 mg I **vitamin C** 148 mg I **vitamin A** 9 mcg.

1 cup (8 fl oz) soy milk

2 kiwis, peeled

⅓ pint (4 oz) strawberries, hulled

⅓ cup (1 oz) sliced almonds, to decorate

ice cubes

A delicious drink, rich in vitamins C and E and fiber. It is also a good source of calcium, and the soy milk is both calming and sleep-inducing.

1 Put all the ingredients in a food processor or blender. Add a few ice cubes, then process until smooth. Pour into a glass and decorate with sliced almonds.

makes 1 cup (8 fl oz)

sleeping beauty

feelin' good

½ **cup (3 oz) blueberries**

1 teaspoon honey

¼ **cup (1 oz) creamed coconut**

½ **cup (4 fl oz) boiling water**

1 small banana

2 tablespoons lime juice

¼ **cup live yogurt**

This creamy concoction has a feel-good factor, but is still amazingly nutritious. Banana provides energy, fiber, and minerals and blueberries are rich in vitamin C.

1 Blend the blueberries with half the honey to a purée and pour into sections of an ice cube tray. Freeze for at least 1 hour.

2 Chop the coconut into pieces and mix with the boiling water until the coconut has dissolved. Leave to cool.

3 Put the banana, lime juice, yogurt, coconut mixture and remaining honey in a blender and blend until completely smooth, scraping the mixture down from the sides of the bowl if necessary.

4 Place the blueberry ice cubes into a tall glass and add the smoothie. Stir lightly so the ice starts to melt.

makes 1 cup (8 fl oz)

NUTRITIONAL CONTENT: energy 427 cals | **calcium** 336 mg | **magnesium** 85 mg | **zinc** 1.8 mg | **vitamin C** 47 mg | **vitamin A** 25 mcg.

beauty fuel

1 orange

¼ lb (4 oz) sugar snap peas, plus extra, sliced, to decorate

½ avocado

2–3 teaspoons lemon juice

mineral water

generous grating of nutmeg

Tired skin will benefit from a regular dose of this avocado smoothie. The sugar snaps and orange juice add tangy goodness, and nutmeg has calming, soothing properties. A good stop-gap between meals.

1 Cut away the peel from the orange and roughly chop the pulp. Push through the juicer with the sugar snap peas. Pour the juice into a blender with the avocado and blend until smooth.

2 Stir in a little lemon juice to taste and add a dash of mineral water if the mixture is too thick. Pour into a glass and add plenty of freshly grated nutmeg and top with finely sliced sugar snaps.

makes 1 cup (8 fl oz)

NUTRITIONAL CONTENT: energy 189 cals | **calcium** 139 mg | **magnesium** 58 mg | **zinc** 1 mg | **vitamin C** 127 mg | **vitamin A** 42 mcg.

169

smooth operator

4 small (8 oz) carrots

½ cup (3½ oz) figs, plus wedges to serve

1 orange

1-inch cube of fresh ginger

1 small (3½ oz) banana

ice cubes

Bananas and figs are rich in tryptophan, necessary for the production of serotonin, which induces a feeling of well-being —great for fighting the winter blues.

1 Juice the carrots, figs, orange and ginger. Put the juice into a blender with the banana and 2 ice cubes and process for 20 seconds for a delicious smoothie. Layer more ice cubes and the fig wedges in a glass, pour the smoothie over them and serve with a stirrer.

makes 1 cup (8 fl oz)

NUTRITIONAL CONTENT: energy 262 cals | calcium 187 mg | magnesium 84 mg | zinc 1.1 mg | vitamin C 88 mg | vitamin A 2256 mcg.

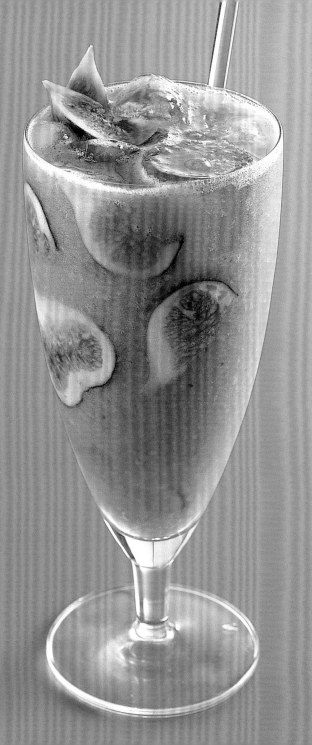

171

NUTRITIONAL CONTENT: energy 75 cals I **calcium** 51 mg I **magnesium** 16 mg I **zinc** 0.2 mg I **vitamin C** 115 mg I **vitamin A** 2107 mcg.

2 carrots

15 g (½ oz) fresh ginger

1 red pepper, seeded

1 leafy celery stalk

ice cubes

Carrots are good for the eyesight because they are rich in vitamin E and betacarotene. Here they are combined with red peppers and ginger, which help to keep infection at bay, and celery, which has an instantly soothing effect. This makes a good all-around supercooler.

1 Push the carrots and ginger, then the pepper, through a juicer. Pour into a glass and serve with the celery stick and several ice cubes.

makes ¾ cup (6 fl oz)

seeing red

peach dream

1 large juicy peach

4 dried apricots

juice of 1 large orange

1 teaspoon honey

2 tablespoons mineral water

¼ cup Greek yogurt

fizzy water (optional) and ice cubes

Smooth and creamy, this is a drink to linger over after a hectic day. Peaches are rich in beta-carotene, which converts to vitamin A, a great nutrient for the skin, complexion and the immune system.

1 Pit and roughly chop the peach and put in a blender with the apricots and orange juice. Blend until smooth, scraping the mixture down from the sides of the bowl if necessary.

2 Stir in the honey and mineral water to thin the consistency slightly. Using a teaspoon, dot the yogurt all around the sides of a tall glass. Pour the peach juice into the glass and swirl the yogurt into the juice with the teaspoon. Top up with fizzy water, if liked, and serve with ice cubes.

makes 1 cup (8 fl oz)

NUTRITIONAL CONTENT: energy 470 cals **| calcium** 366 mg **| magnesium** 90 mg **| zinc** 1.6 mg **| vitamin C** 96 mg **| vitamin A** 326 mcg.

175

bean good

⅔ cup (2 oz) broccoli

1 apple

1 pear

3 oz bean sprouts

ice cubes

The combination of calcium, minerals and vitamins contained in broccoli makes this a great tonic for hair, teeth and bones. Combined with apples, pears and bean sprouts, this is a blend to put you in mint condition. Use the ingredients straight from the refrigerator so they are refreshingly cold.

1 Cut the broccoli, apple and pear into pieces and push through the juicer with the bean sprouts. Pour into a glass and serve immediately over ice.

makes 1 cup (8 fl oz)

NUTRITIONAL CONTENT: energy 147 cals | **calcium** 64 mg | **magnesium** 40 mg | **zinc** 0.8 mg | **vitamin C** 64 mg | **vitamin A** 60 mcg.

rosy glow

½ **red apple**

3 rosemary sprigs, plus extra, to serve

½ **teaspoon herb honey**

1 cup (8 fl oz) boiling water

squeeze of lemon juice

Rosemary stimulates the circulation and soothes aching joints by increasing blood supply. It's also very good for promoting healthy hair. Rosemary is delicious with almost any fruit and this apple tea is particularly soothing. To reap all the benefits, eat the apple slices afterward.

1 Core the apple and cut into thick slices. Put in a cup or teapot with the rosemary and honey and add the boiling water. Leave to infuse for 4–5 minutes and add the lemon juice before serving.

makes 1 cup (8 fl oz)

NUTRITIONAL CONTENT: energy 37 cals | **calcium** 10 mg | **magnesium** 4 mg | **zinc** 0.1 mg | **vitamin C** 5 mg | **vitamin A** 3 mcg.

179

soothing brew

**3 chamomile flowerheads or
1 chamomile tea bag**

**1 lemon verbena flower spray,
plus 2 leaves**

½ teaspoon honey

1 cup (8 fl oz) boiling water

lemon slice, to serve

Chamomile tea is most frequently drunk as a late-night soother, but also aids digestion and treats anxiety and nerves. Here it is combined with lemon verbena, which also has calming properties.

1 Put the chamomile and verbena in a cup with the honey and add the boiling water. Leave to infuse for 4–5 minutes (no longer or the tea might become bitter). Serve with a slice of lemon.

makes 1 cup (8 fl oz)

NUTRITIONAL CONTENT: energy 14 cals | **calcium** 4 mg | **magnesium** 2 mg | **zinc** 0 mg | **vitamin C** 0 mg | **vitamin A** 0 mcg.

181

NUTRITIONAL CONTENT: **energy** 14 cals I **calcium** 4 mg I **magnesium** 2 mg I **zinc** 0 mg I **vitamin C** 0 mg I **vitamin A** 0 mcg.

3 sprigs lavender

½ teaspoon honey

1 cup (8 fl oz) boiling water

Lavender tea relaxes the mind and body and helps to achieve a good night's sleep. The flavor is an acquired taste, so add a squeeze of lemon juice or infuse some pared orange rind with the flowers if you like.

1 Put the lavender sprigs in a cup with their stalk ends uppermost so they can easily be lifted out. Add the honey and boiling water and leave to infuse for 4–5 minutes before serving.

makes 1 cup (8 fl oz)

pillow talk

eat your greens

1 savoy cabbage

2 large onions

4 garlic cloves

2 14½-oz cans chopped tomatoes

2 green peppers

2 celery sticks

6 carrots

½ lb (8 oz) green beans, sliced

2–3 tablespoons vegetable bouillon powder

oregano and thyme

2½ cups (20 fl oz) vegetable stock

pepper

Cabbage soup is a healthy and effective way to help you lose weight, as well as making a nutritious detoxifying soup that is excellent for cleansing the colon and ridding the body of toxins. Be aware that this diet approach should be undertaken only under medical supervision, and is certainly no substitute for a healthy balanced diet. Try varying the texture and the seasonings to keep the inevitable feelings of monotony at bay.

1 Put all the ingredients into a large pan. Bring to a boil and reduce to a simmer until the vegetables are soft. Add a little water if the soup looks too thick. Season to taste with pepper and serve hot or cold.

makes 10 small servings

NUTRITIONAL CONTENT: **energy** 80 cals | **protein** 4 g | **fat** 1 g | **carbohydrate** 15 g | **calcium** 86 mg | **iron** 1.9 mg | **vitamin C** 85 mg.

185

summer soup

1½ lbs ripe nectarines, peeled and pitted

1 cup (8 fl oz) freshly squeezed grapefruit juice

½ cup (4 fl oz) white grape juice or dry white wine

¼ teaspoon Tabasco sauce

1 tablespoon balsamic vinegar

2 tablespoons chopped fresh cilantro

salt and pepper

Nectarines are low in calories, yet one large nectarine provides almost three-quarters of the daily vitamin C requirement. The fruit has a gentle laxative effect and is also rich in iron and potassium.

1 Purée the nectarines in a food processor with the grapefruit juice, grape juice or wine, Tabasco sauce and balsamic vinegar. Add salt and pepper to taste.

2 Chop the cilantro roughly and add to the nectarine mixture, then cover and chill. Serve the soup in small bowls or cups.

serves 4

NUTRITIONAL CONTENT: energy 111 cals I **protein** 3 g I **fat** 1 g I **carbohydrate** 26 g I **calcium** 31 mg I **iron** 1.2 mg I **vitamin C** 90 mg.

NUTRITIONAL CONTENT: energy 158 cals I protein 15 g I fat 3 g I carbohydrate 16 g I calcium 212 mg I iron 6.8 mg I vitamin C 18 mg.

3 lbs mussels

¾ cup (6 fl oz) dry white wine

4 shallots, finely chopped

4 cups (32 fl oz) canned coconut milk

½ tablespoon finely chopped fresh ginger

3 plum tomatoes, skinned, seeded and roughly chopped

2 large chilies, seeded and chopped

¼ cup canned sweet corn kernels

to garnish

1 green onion, finely sliced

2 tablespoons basil leaves

Seafood is universally hailed as brain food and, as it is high in zinc, it is a beneficial addition to the diet when stress levels are high. Zinc helps to break down alcohol and is a vital component of insulin, which controls blood sugar levels.

1 Wash the mussels in cold water. Pull off their beards and discard any mussels that are open and do not close when tapped on a hard surface.

2 Put the wine and shallots into a large saucepan and boil for about 2–3 minutes. Add the mussels and boil for 2 minutes, or until all the mussels have opened. Immediately drain them over a bowl. As soon as they are cool enough to handle, carefully pull them from their shells, discarding any that have not opened. Reserve the broth and the mussels.

3 Strain the mussel broth into a large pan, discarding any grit or dirt that may have sunk to the bottom. Add the coconut milk, ginger, tomatoes, chilies and sweet corn. Heat and simmer for 2 minutes, then add the mussels.

4 Serve the soup in warmed bowls sprinkled with green onions and basil leaves.

serves 6

mussel power

juicy lucy

½ lb (8 oz) watermelon chunks

**⅔ pint (7 oz) strawberries, plus
extra to decorate**

1 mint sprig, to decorate

Watermelon is the ideal detoxifier, the flesh is packed with
beta-carotene and vitamin C. By adding strawberries, you'll
be receiving a great boost of vitamin C as well as helping
fight bacteria in your system. This juice is rich in zinc and
potassium, two great eliminators.

1 Juice the fruit and process in a blender with a couple of
ice cubes. Serve decorated with a sprig of mint and the
extra strawberries.

makes 1 cup (8 fl oz)

NUTRITIONAL CONTENT: energy 116 cals I **calcium** 46 mg I **magnesium** 36 mg I **zinc** 0.6 mg I
vitamin C 170 mg I **vitamin A** 79 mcg.

191

flush-a-bye-baby

½ lb (8 oz) cranberries

½ lb (8 oz) watermelon or honeydew melon chunks, plus sticks to serve

1 small (8 oz) cucumber

The cucumber in this juice provides protective antioxidants for the digestive tract and, combined with the melon, acts as a diuretic to cleanse the intestinal system. Good for cystitis.

1 Juice all the ingredients together, including the seeds of the melon and the skin of the cucumber. Serve in a tumbler and decorate with a couple of melon sticks.

makes 1 cup (8 fl oz)

NUTRITIONAL CONTENT: energy 140 cals I **calcium** 93 mg I **magnesium** 58 mg I **zinc** 1.3 mg I **vitamin C** 58 mg I **vitamin A** 131 mcg.

194

NUTRITIONAL CONTENT: energy 142 cals I **calcium** 156 mg I **magnesium** 34 mg I **zinc** 0.9 mg I **vitamin C** 96 mg I **vitamin A** 197 mcg.

1 medium (8 oz) pear

⅛ small (4 oz) cabbage

1 medium (2 oz) celery stalk, plus a stalk, to decorate

1 oz watercress

ice cubes

Cabbage is a great detoxifier. It aids digestion and prevents fluid retention and constipation. Watercress is a powerful intestinal cleanser, the cabbage and the pear rid the colon of waste matter and the celery purifies the lymph.

1 Juice all the ingredients together and serve in a glass over ice, decorated with a celery stick.

makes 1 cup (8 fl oz)

spring clean

squeaky green

3 small (6 oz) carrots

2 medium (3 oz) celery stalks

¼ lb (4 oz) spinach

¼ lb (4 oz) lettuce

2 tablespoons (1 oz) parsley, plus extra to decorate

ice cubes

This juice will prevent the build-up of toxins in your system, which leads to sluggish metabolism, low energy and possibly serious illnesses. Carrots, lettuce, spinach and celery all work to regenerate the liver and lymph system and aid digestion. Parsley is good for kidney stones.

1 Juice the ingredients and process in a blender with a couple of ice cubes. Decorate with sprigs of parsley.

makes 1 cup (8 fl oz)

NUTRITIONAL CONTENT: energy 106 cals | **calcium** 344 mg | **magnesium** 86 mg | **zinc** 1.5 mg | **vitamin C** 93 mg | **vitamin A** 2379 mcg.

197

orchard medley

12 (3 oz) pitted dried plums

¼ pint (3½ oz) blackberries

½ cup (4 fl oz) apple juice

1 teaspoon honey

1 apple wedge, to decorate

You can make this detoxifying smoothie at any time of year as frozen blackberries make a good substitute for fresh. Juice your own apples or use a good quality tart apple juice to counteract the sweetness of the dried plums.

1 Put the prunes and blackberries in a blender and blend until smooth, scraping the mixture down from the sides of the bowl if necessary.

2 Add the apple juice and blend until completely smooth. Taste and add a little honey if the mixture is too tart. Serve in a tall glass, decorated with an apple wedge.

makes 1 cup (8 fl oz)

NUTRITIONAL CONTENT: **energy** 192 cals I **calcium** 74 mg I **magnesium** 46 mg I **zinc** 0.6 mg I **vitamin C** 29 mg I **vitamin A** 31 mcg.

199

tropical trio

½ small mango, peeled, plus a wedge to decorate

1 thick slice of pineapple, peeled

½ small papaya

juice of ½ orange

squeeze of lime juice

Mango, pineapple and papaya are packed with beta-carotene and vitamin C and make a delicious detox blend. This quantity makes one tall drink but you can make a larger batch for a chilled supply.

1 Roughly chop the mango and pineapple and put in a blender. Discard the seeds from the papaya and scoop the flesh into the blender.

2 Add the orange and lime juice and blend until completely smooth, scraping the mixture down from the sides of the bowl if necessary. Serve in a tall glass, decorated with a wedge of mango.

makes 1 cup (8 fl oz)

NUTRITIONAL CONTENT: energy 138 cals I **calcium** 57 mg I **magnesium** 37 mg I **zinc** 0.6 mg I **vitamin C** 147 mg I **vitamin A** 326 mcg.

201

strawberry cleanser

½ cup (4 fl oz) cranberries or ½ cup (4 fl oz) unsweetened cranberry juice

⅓ pint (4 oz) strawberries

½ cup (3½ oz) seedless red or black grapes

Cranberries are renowned for their cleansing properties and, like all red fruits, are packed with vitamin C and cancer-fighting chemicals. For best results make this smoothie when strawberries are at their sweetest and juiciest, otherwise you might need to add a little honey to sweeten.

1 If using whole cranberries, push them through a juicer. Pour the juice into a blender or food processor.

2 Hull the strawberries and put in the blender with the grapes. Blend until smooth, scraping the mixture down from the sides of the bowl if necessary. Serve immediately.

makes 1 cup (8 fl oz)

NUTRITIONAL CONTENT: energy 143 cals I **calcium** 33 mg I **magnesium** 20 mg I **zinc** 0.2 mg I **vitamin C** 129 mg I **vitamin A** 5 mcg.

lemon barley water

rind of 1 unwaxed lemon, cut into fine strips, plus extra to decorate

2 tablespoons barley

5 cups (40 fl oz) boiling water

sugar, to taste

ice cubes

What could be more soothing and relaxing than the fresh taste of homemade lemon barley water—a perfect summer detox drink at the end of a tiring day.

1 Put the lemon rind into a heatproof jar with the barley. Cover with the boiling water and stir well. Cover and let stand overnight.

2 Add sugar to taste, then strain the barley water through a piece of muslin—the liquid should be clear.

3 To serve, fill glasses with ice cubes, pour in the lemon barley water and decorate with fine strips of lemon rind.

makes 5 cups (40 fl oz)

NUTRITIONAL CONTENT: energy 85 cals | **calcium** 6 mg | **magnesium** 7 mg | **zinc** 0.2 mg | **vitamin C** 3 mg | **vitamin A** 0 mcg.

205

red devil

2 small (4 oz) beets

1 carrot

½ mild red chili

1 orange

crushed ice

Beets are a good blood-builder and an excellent cleanser for the intestine and liver. They are also rich in calcium, vitamin C and minerals. Oranges and carrots are also vital ingredients for a detox diet, so keep a fresh supply.

1 Roughly chop the beets, carrot and chili. Cut away the peel from the orange and roughly chop the flesh. Push the beets, carrot and chili, then the orange, through a juicer. Serve with crushed ice.

makes 1 cup (8 fl oz)

NUTRITIONAL CONTENT: energy 132 cals I **calcium** 120 mg I **magnesium** 33 mg I **zinc** 0.7 mg I **vitamin C** 102 mg I **vitamin A** 889 mcg.

NUTRITIONAL CONTENT: energy 113 cals | calcium 54 mg | magnesium 17 mg | zinc 0.3 mg | vitamin C 16 mg | vitamin A 13 mcg.

2 celery sticks

1 crisp apple

½ cup (3½ oz) green grapes

ice cubes

This drink contains three very effective cleansers in one tall cooler, and it's easy enough on the tastebuds to drink on a regular basis. All the ingredients provide vitamin C.

1 Chop the celery sticks and apple and push through the juicer with the grapes. Serve with plenty of ice cubes.

makes 1 cup (8 fl oz)

freshen up

herbal harmony

3–4 parsley sprigs

3–4 mint sprigs

½ oz fresh ginger, peeled

1 cup (8 fl oz) boiling water

1 teaspoon lavender honey

This combination may sound unusual, but it will give you a thoroughly good cleanse. Parsley is rich in vitamins and iron and is a diuretic herb, used in the treatment of fluid retention. Ginger and mint are both good for digestion and give the infusion a lift.

1 Put the parsley and mint sprigs, including the stalks, in a cup. Thinly slice the ginger and add to the cup with the boiling water.

2 Leave to infuse for 4–5 minutes then lift out the herbs and ginger, if desired. Stir in a little honey to taste.

makes 1 cup (8 fl oz)

NUTRITIONAL CONTENT: energy 33 cals | calcium 20 mg | magnesium 1 mg | zinc 0.1 mg | vitamin C 9 mg | vitamin A 33 mcg.

211

digestive duo

½ fennel bulb plus stalks to decorate

1 juicy pear

½ cup (4 fl oz) boiling water

Fennel and pear work well together, not only in flavor but because they're both effective diuretics and digestive aids. Pears also contain pectin, which helps flush out toxins from the body.

1 Roughly chop the fennel and pear into pieces and push through the juicer. Pour the juice into a small pan and add the boiling water. Heat gently until hot but not boiling and pour into a cup.

makes 1 cup (8 fl oz)

NUTRITIONAL CONTENT: energy 72 cals | **calcium** 41 mg | **magnesium** 19 mg | **zinc** 0.7 mg | **vitamin C** 14 mg | **vitamin A** 28 mcg.

213

dynamic detox

8 dandelion leaves, torn into pieces

1 cup (8 fl oz) boiling water

1 tablespoon lemon juice

2 teaspoons honey

Dandelion leaves are one of the most effective detox foods, powerfully diuretic but rich in the essential minerals that might be lost during a detox regime. Lemon, like all citrus fruits, is a good cleanser and packed with vital vitamins.

1 Put the dandelion leaves in a cup and cover with boiling water. Leave to infuse for 4 minutes then lift out the leaves. Stir in the lemon juice and honey and serve.

makes 1 cup (8 fl oz)

NUTRITIONAL CONTENT: energy 53 cals I **calcium** 24 mg I **magnesium** 8 mg I **zinc** 0.2 mg I **vitamin C** 5 mg I **vitamin A** 7 mcg.

215

minty magic

1 large Spanish onion, chopped

2 garlic cloves, roughly chopped

½ lb (8 oz) leeks, roughly chopped

6 cups (48 fl oz) chicken or vegetable stock

8 oz canned butter beans

1 thyme sprig

1 bay leaf

½ lb (8 oz) snow peas

1 bunch of mint, leaves removed from the stalks

salt and pepper

to garnish

1 tablespoon sour cream

2 tablespoons caviar or fish roe, black or red

Peas and beans are very high in fiber and detoxify the digestive system. The onion, leek and garlic will help purify the blood and vital organs.

1 Sauté the onion, garlic and leeks with a little stock, covered, in a large saucepan until softened. Add the butter beans, remaining stock and the thyme and bay leaf and boil for 10 minutes, then reduce the heat and simmer gently for 20 minutes.

2 Add the snow peas and the mint leaves, reserving a few leaves for garnish, and boil for 5 minutes. Transfer to a food processor and blend until smooth.

3 Pass the soup through a fine sieve, return to the pan and season with salt and pepper to taste. Serve the soup in warmed bowls, with a swirl of sour cream and a dollop of caviar or fish roe. Finish each bowl with a mint leaf and serve immediately.

serves 4

NUTRITIONAL CONTENT: energy 176 cals I **protein** 12 g I **fat** 3 g I **carbohydrate** 27 g I **calcium** 104 mg I **iron** 4 mg I **vitamin C** 48 mg.

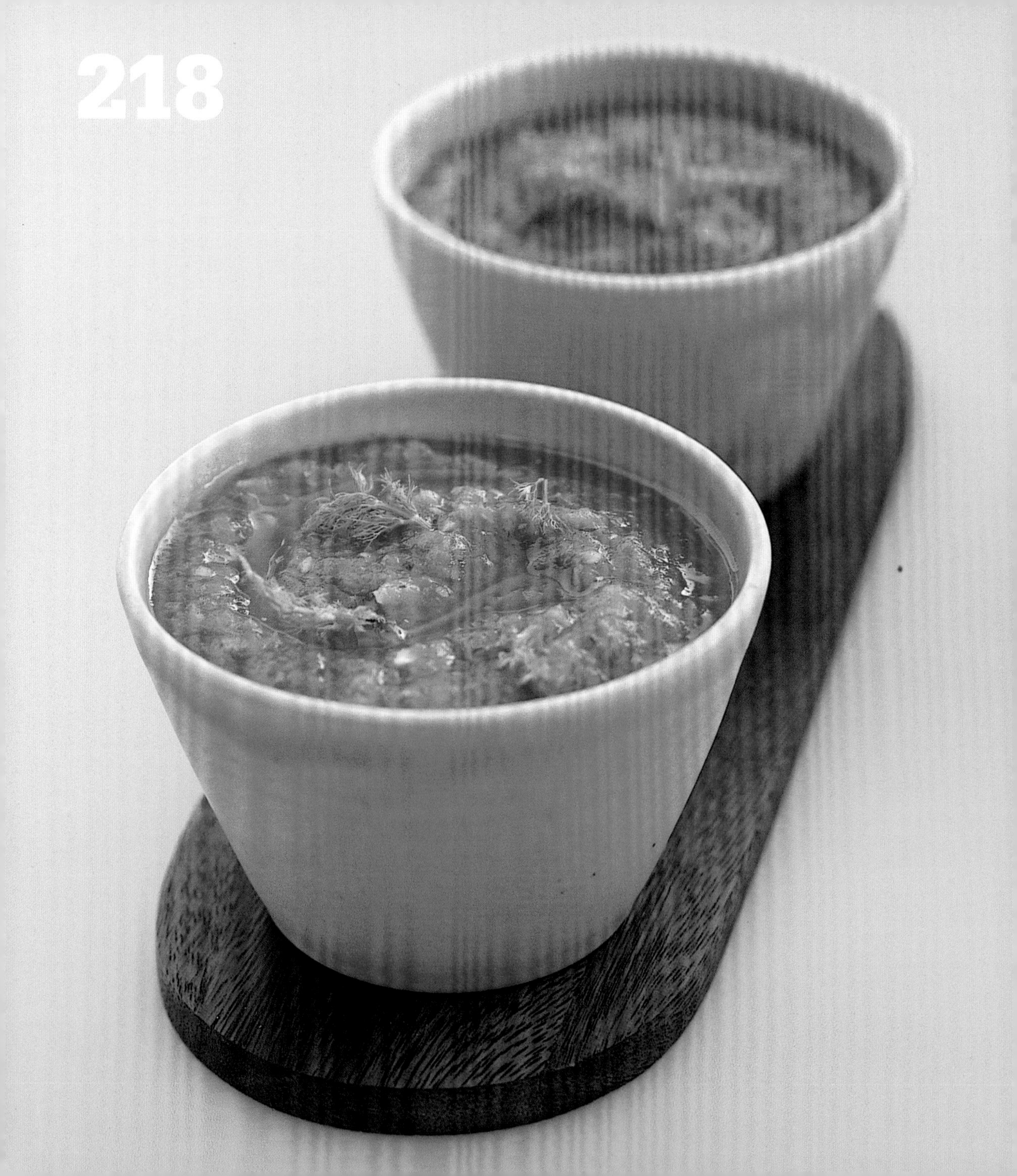

NUTRITIONAL CONTENT: energy 70 cals | protein 2 g | fat 4 g | carbohydrate 8 g | calcium 34 mg | iron 1.3 mg | vitamin C 37 mg.

1½ lbs ripe red tomatoes

1 large fennel bulb

1 cup (8 fl oz) boiling water

1 teaspoon rock salt

¾ teaspoon coriander seeds

½ teaspoon mixed peppercorns

1 tablespoon extra virgin olive oil

1 large garlic clove, crushed

1 small onion, chopped

1 tablespoon balsamic vinegar

1 tablespoon lemon juice

1 teaspoon tomato purée

¾ teaspoon chopped oregano

This light, vitamin-packed soup is ideal for a summer detox and perfect for boosting the immune system. Fennel is a natural diuretic and is also rich in phytoestrogens. It is good for calming hot flashes.

1 Plunge the tomatoes into a large pan of boiling water and leave for about 1 minute. Drain and remove the skins, then chop roughly.

2 Trim the green fronds from the fennel and reserve. Thinly slice the bulb and put it into a saucepan with the boiling water and the rock salt. Cover and simmer for 10 minutes.

3 Crush the coriander seeds and peppercorns using a mortar and pestle. Heat the olive oil in a large saucepan and add the crushed spices, garlic and onion. Cook gently for 5 minutes.

4 Add the balsamic vinegar, lemon juice, tomatoes and oregano and stir well. Add the fennel with its cooking liquid and the tomato purée. Bring to a simmer and let cook uncovered for 30 minutes.

5 Blend the soup to a purée in a food processor. Let it cool then chill for at least 2 hours. Serve the soup garnished with the reserved fennel fronds.

serves 4

feel-good fennel

orient express

4 cups water

3 oz dashi granules

3½ oz miso

**1 tablespoon mirin or
dry sherry**

8 oz firm tofu, cut into cubes

to garnish

1 green onion, diagonally sliced

**1 sheet of toasted nori seaweed,
crumbled into small pieces**

Miso is a soy bean paste; it contains powerful isoflavones and is thought to protect against breast and prostate cancer. Soy-rich foods are also believed to reduce LDL (bad cholesterol). Dashi is a Japanese fish-based stock.

1 Using a wooden spoon, combine the water and dashi granules in a small saucepan, then bring the mixture to the boil. Reduce the heat to medium, add the miso and mirin and stir to combine; be sure that the mixture does not boil, as overheating will result in a loss of flavor.

2 Add the tofu cubes to the hot stock and heat without boiling over medium heat for 5 minutes. Serve in warm bowls sprinkled with the green onion and nori.

serves 4

NUTRITIONAL CONTENT: energy 108 cals | **protein** 10 g | **fat** 4 g | **carbohydrate** 6 g | **calcium** 360 mg | **iron** 2.8 mg | **vitamin C** 1 mg.

221

index

223

acknowledgments

Executive Editor: Sarah Ford
Project Editor: Kate Tuckett
Executive Art Editor: Geoff Fennell
Designer: Sue Michniewicz
Photographer: Stephen Conroy
Stylist: Angela Swaffield
Home Economists: Joanna Farrow, David Morgan
Production Controller: Aileen O'Reilly